GBC

GOVERNMENT BEYOND THE CENTRE

SERIES EDITOR: GERRY STOKER

The world of sub-central government and administration – including local authorities, quasi-governmental bodies and the agencies of public-private partnerships – has seen massive changes in recent years and is at the heart of the current restructuring of government in the United Kingdom and other Western democracies.

The intention of the *Government Beyond the Centre* series is to bring the study of this often-neglected world into the mainstream of social science research, applying the spotlight of critical analysis to what has traditionally been the preserve of institutional public administration approaches.

Its focus is on the agenda of change currently being faced by sub-central government, the economic, political and ideological forces that underlie it, and the structures of power and influence that are emerging. Its objective is to provide up-to-date and informative accounts of the new forms of government, management and administration that are emerging.

The series will be of interest to students and practitioners of politics, public and social administration, and all those interested in the reshaping of the governmental institutions which have a daily and major impact on our lives.

GOVERNMENT BEYOND THE CENTRE

SERIES EDITOR: GERRY STOKER

Series Standing Order

If you would like to receive future titles in this series as they are published, you can make use of our standing order facility. To place a standing order please contact your bookseller or, in case of difficulty, write to us at the address below with your name and address and the name of the series. Please state with which title you wish to begin your standing order. (If you live outside the UK we may not have the rights for your area, in which case we will forward your order to the publisher concerned.)

Standing Order Service, Macmillan Distribution Ltd, Houndmills, Basingstoke, Hampshire, RG21 2XS, England

Managing in
Local Government

Richard Kerley

MACMILLAN

First published 1994 by
THE MACMILLAN PRESS LTD
Houndmills, Basingstoke, Hampshire RG21 2XS
and London
Companies and representatives
throughout the world

ISBN 0–333–60467–9 hardcover
ISBN 0–333–60468–7 paperback

A catalogue record for this book is available
from the British Library.

Copy-edited and typeset by Povey–Edmondson
Okehampton and Rochdale, England

Printed in Hong Kong

To Liam and Sandra

Contents

List of Tables and Figures

Tables

Figures

Note: The terms used in this book refer to: Scotland, England, England
and Wales. Great Britain is the term used for all three countries and the
phrase the United Kingdom includes Northern Ireland.

Acknowledgements

The idea for this book, and many of the ideas that are contained within it, arise from my work over almost twenty years with literally hundreds of local government officials and councillors. In some cases they may have learnt something from me; I have learnt a great deal more from them. Fortunately for some of them it is not possible to list all their names, but I am very grateful to them all.

Different parts of the text have benefited from being read in draft and commented on by a number of local authority officials and other colleagues. My thanks to David Dorward, Mike Enston, Keith Jackson, Arthur McCourt, Bobby Mackie, Trevor Muir, and Vicki Nash. My thanks also to the series editor, Gerry Stoker and my publisher Steven Kennedy.

My immediate colleagues, Alan Alexander, John Fairley, Lewis Gunn, Kevin Orr, Val Wilson and Douglas Wynn, have discussed some of the ideas in this book with me – they agree with some of those ideas, and not with others. Some of the bulk wordprocessing has been done by Samantha Lockhart, Bess Taylor, Jaqueline Mulligan and Peter Kimpston. My family have tolerated a great deal of lost time and occasional tantrums from me. They have nonetheless coped patiently as I struggled along, and have made helpful comments on the work.

Despite all this assistance, the errors of commission and omission – of which there are no doubt many – are entirely mine.

University of Strathclyde   RICHARD KERLEY

The author and publishers wish to thank the following for permission to reproduce copyright material: HMSO for Figure 9.1, Strathclyde Region for permission to adapt Figure 5.1; and the London Borough of Ealing for permission to adapt Figure 7.1.

Introduction

'A government ill executed, whatever it might be in theory must be in practice a poor government.' — Alexander Hamilton, 1787

This book is about the way in which local government is run in Britain. It is written for those who are involved in running local government and those who are interested in how it works.

The way in which local government works is changing dramatically and rapidly. The reasons for that change are many and various, and they are explored in the first section of the book, Chapters 1 and 2. The change is significant: 'From being a quiet backwater of routine administration and parochial politics, local government has been pushed into the limelight' (Stoker, 1991, p. xiv).

Such changes have forced local government to think not simply about what services it provides, but about the way in which it provides them. This has in turn forced members and officers to think about what they do, and the way they work within the organisation. Education officials who have been accustomed to telling schools what to do – and what not to do – now find they are obliged to negotiate with school governors and school boards. Finance officials have to adjust to service departments asking what a particular financial service will cost, and whether it compares favourably with the service offered by the local bank. Members have had to adjust to the idea that a separation between client and contractor means their request for 'a little extra work in the local park' is now a contract variation. Through all of this, managers and senior staff in every council find they are facing challenges and dilemmas for which their initial training did not equip them. They are being expected to operate as *managers*, not as social workers, planners, architects or accountants.

To exchange the certainty of professional expertise for the uncertainty of management is a difficult transition, and one that some people never make successfully. The way in which this transition is made, and its implications for the role of manager within a council, are explained and discussed in Chapter 3. Managing the resources of the organisation more effectively is covered in Chapters 4 to 6. The purpose of effective management in local government is further explored and developed in Chapters 7 and 8. The argument advanced is that the shift toward a more outward-oriented and consumer-led view of what services local government should provide and how it should provide them will actually help local government to prepare for a greater emphasis on its role as 'government' and not simply as provider of services. Chapter 9 considers the role of councillors in the management of the council, and considers the changing relationship between councillors and managers. Chapter 10 takes a look at the future of management in local government.

This book is written for people who are doing the kind of jobs which are described, discussed and analysed here. It is also written for those who work with these people and are interested in the work that they do. It is not in any sense an open learning text, but there are points in the text where the reader is asked to pause and think about some aspects of local government practice he or she has observed. At the end of each chapter are prompt questions to help *you* think about the way you have seen these changes affecting local government. This is intended as a means of encouraging thought about some of the practical consequences of the theoretical or general issues raised. A good reader interrogates a book whilst working through it – here the book also interrogates the reader.

This book is written on the basis that we cannot simply refer to 'managers' in local government as though they are an undifferentiated, homogeneous mass, anymore than in industry and commerce. The text therefore distinguishes at numerous points between operational managers, support managers and those with strategic management responsibilities. They all have individually demanding roles, but of course need to integrate their work effectively in order to achieve the desired results for the organisation. As Hamilton in effect observed, if they do not perform effectively, then the fine sentiments of council and committee debate remain just that.

The examples cited in the text are drawn from councils in Scotland, where I principally work, and from authorities in

England and Wales. In some instances I have not given the name of the council from which the example is drawn, nor have I at any point named any of those who have spoken to me about their work as managers or members. The individual anonymity reflects the desire of some of those staff and councillors who were interviewed not to have their views attributed. In some cases I have not named the council where a particular practice is described because, while there are few councils that are direct competitors with each other, there are many which are in a sense 'comparative competitors', and to record a particular practice as being carried out in Council X is to invite the observation 'typical of them' – a comment which in some ways indicates how parochial local government can still be.

1 Public Management: Fashion or Fixture?

One week before the General Election of 1992 an article in *The Independent* newspaper was headlined 'A Revolution That Will Go On' (Hughes, 1992). The 'revolution' referred to was the changes in public service management that had occurred over the term of the previous three Conservative governments: 'Thirteen years of Conservative government have revolutionised the shape and style of management in the national public sector. From the Met Office to English Heritage . . . senior civil servants routinely speak about customers and markets . . . they run their own budgets, and implement their own devolved decisions.' The author's conclusion that 'the Public Service Managerial Revolution will go on' appears unassailable. But is it? In this first chapter, we assess the extent to which the increased emphasis on managerial effectiveness in the public services is a phenomenon that will persist, and the degree to which it will continue to be influential. The particular concern of this book is with the changing nature of management in local government. However, the changes that have been – and continue to be – seen in local government are best viewed against the context of an ongoing debate on the management of public services generally. That debate also reflects a continuing lively discussion about the nature of the management process as a whole, and whether it has common elements and forms both within the private and public sectors and between them.

It is important, therefore, to consider whether the increased emphasis on the importance of effective management is likely to be a continuing feature of our analysis of public services or whether it is a fashion whose importance will fade over time.

Managing public services – a phenomenon of this decade?

Shortly after his appointment as Secretary of State for the Environment in the 1979 Conservative government, Michael Heseltine wrote about his views on the relationship between ministers and management. 'Efficient Management is a key to the national revival . . . and the management ethos must run right through our national life – public and private companies, the civil service, nationalised industries, local government, the National Health Service' (Heseltine, 1980, p. 62). Despite the slightly messianic quality of this phrase, one consistent feature of Mr Heseltine's ministerial career has been his continuing concern with the way in which the machinery of government actually runs. In effect, he has for a long time argued that the broad policies of change must be matched with processes of decision-making and managerial control that ensure such policies actually are put into effect. At a time when he was introducing MINIS – Management Information System for Ministers – into the Department of the Environment he outlined as good a working definition of the 'management process' as we are likely to find in any textbook: ' – setting clear objectives; – a strategy to reach those objectives; – a method of monitoring progress to ensure one is not loosing momentum or, if one is, that one can adjust to new circumstances deliberately and quickly' (p. 62).

On occasion, and on this matter in particular, he appears to have found himself in a minority within the Cabinet, and there are some amusing accounts of the way in which he persistently and often unsuccessfully tried to persuade fellow ministers to adopt some of his approaches to the management process. The significance of this is not to highlight the personal enthusiasms of one minister, but to contrast this episode with the degree to which, by the end of the 1980s, the language of 'management', 'managing' and 'managers' had entered the everyday vocabulary of politicians and officials in central and local government.

Compare two example: one from central government and one from a regional council in Scotland. The head of the Home Civil Service gives a clear indication of the Whitehall view in his foreword to *A Guide for New Managers* (HM Government, 1990a): 'The purpose of this book is to help you to be a successful manager. Today's Civil Service places much more emphasis on management of people, resources and the delivery of services. . . If you are a good manager, you will achieve more.'

A recent annual report of Lothian Regional Council (Lothian Region Council, 1992) has the leader of the Labour Group writing in the language of management that: 'The Council needs to ensure that

. . . it is able to respond to changing circumstances and priorities. . . It is through this [strategic] framework that the Council will seek to direct its corporate affairs, set priorities, allocate resources.'

As we entered the 1990s, a concern for the way in which public services were managed and run was commonplace among both Conservative politicians and their opponents in both Labour and Liberal Democratic parties. In all three major parties there were to be found members and elected representatives asserting the view that improvement in the management of public services was certainly as important as additional resources being committed to those services. Although this emphasis on the improvement of management in the public services re-emerged in the 1980s, it should not be seen as a recent phenomenon. Previous postwar British governments have attempted to tackle the way in which central government is managed as well as the internal management of local government. They have also made efforts to review the alleged staffing deficiencies of local government during the years of marked growth in local services and facilities. The last reorganisation of local government both in England and Wales and in Scotland saw considerable emphasis on the manner on which the new authorities were to be managed. This can best be seen as a reaction to the near paralysis and resistance to organisational change which affected local government on both sides of the border during the 1950s and 1960s, a situation which is described in the writings of some of the ministers involved. What occasionally comes through from some of the ministerial observers is a sense of near despair at the state in which they find some of the local authorities, and their limited capacity for delivering those central policy initiatives. Richard Crossman describes the perspective from the ministry:

The councillors are an attractive group but, oh dear, their borough engineer was dim to the nth degree and the general body of their officials drearily incompetent. Apart from the borough treasurer there was really no quality at all, and I began to realise that one of the problems of local government is the real, inherent weaknesses of administration (Crossman, 1975, p. 123).

If we look back further than the postwar decades we can find examples of a concern for the management of public services. Even at a time when there was a far more constrained view of what the public services should do, and the range of services for which they should be responsible, there was often a concomitant concern to ensure that those services and facilities were provided more effectively; in effect, that they were better managed. As Stanyer (1976, p. 234) observed in his overview of management traditions in local government, that thinking was not usually advanced or well developed. 'The development of management thinking in public administration occurred later than in most private commercial and industrial organisations, and this has given the management movement in local government some of its characteristic features.'

A concern for the effectiveness of public service management is not a phenomenon confined to the 1980s – though it is particularly pronounced during this period – and it is not a political experience confined to any one country. The initial impetus for change in the USSR initiated by Mikhail Gorbachev at this time comprised a number of streams of development, one of which was perestroika or restructuring, which was intended to achieve significant reforms in the management of the economy and of society.

The Organisation for Economic Cooperation and Development (OECD) carried out a study in the late 1980s of trends in public management across a number of developed industrial societies. In all of those countries there were common themes that characterised changes in public policy. Some of the trends studied were of long-term significance in many large industrial societies, and included a common desire to reduce levels of public expenditure by, for example, seeking to reduce the size of the public sector. Across all the countries studied, 'Raising public sector efficiency and effectiveness via management reform appears now to be firmly placed on all government agendas' (OECD, 1989, p. 1).

The impact of the search for enhanced effectiveness in the public services has often been controversial. In the health service and in local government there have been many critics of the increased emphasis on management and the enhanced role of managers, in contrast to the tradition of cultural and organisational dominance by professional service-providers. This has particularly been the case when such changes have been combined with cash-limited expenditure, reductions in expenditure, or limits on growth of expenditure – three distinct and different phenomena, which have sometimes been combined or confused by critics. Within the public services as a whole, and within local government itself, there has been a lively debate about the characteristics of the effective manager and the balance between that emphasis on managerial concerns and the traditional professional base of local government senior staff. Even among academic commentators and observers analysis is often flavoured with scepticism, with one major review (Hood, 1991) suggesting a parallel between 'new public management' and the emperor's new clothes.

Public and private management – similar or different?

The latter half of the nineteenth century and the whole of this century have seen the continuing growth in both size and complexity of the wide range of public services that we all now assume to be an inherent characteristic of any advanced society. The extent to which that growth has altered the balance of our gross domestic product in the United Kingdom can be seen in Figure 1.1.

FIGURE 1.1   Total public expenditure as % of GDP

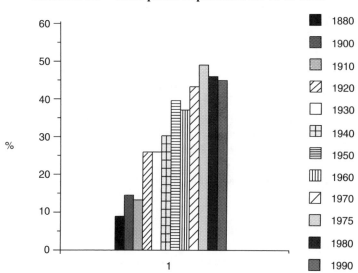

Sources: Ward 1988; and National Income and Expenditure, various.

Over that same period of time, the increasing complexity and organisational demands associated with the change in scale and nature of industrial and commercial organisations has seen the growth of management in employment and as an academic discipline.

Throughout this period, a consistent and recurrent feature of academic debate has been the similarities and differences between management in the trading sector and in public services, and what characteristics management in each environment has in common. The public consequence of that unresolved debate has often been a prescriptive assertion that public services would generally be more effectively run if 'business like' methods were employed in running them. This idea of an inherently more efficient form of management practised in the private sector has seen frequent expression in the temptation of all governments to invite 'businessmen' to lend their qualities and apply their disciplines to the organisation of various public services and activities. Haldane was called in during the First World War; Geddes during the political and financial crises of the 1930s. Beaverbrook and Woolton were asked to assist the Churchill governments of World War II and the early 1950s. The major enthusiasm for institutional and economic reform expressed by the 1970 Conservative government saw the introduction of the then President of the CBI from outside the House of Commons straight into a cabinet position. Labour governments have turned to managers who have created their reputations in the private sector in order to try to turn around loss-making public enterprise (Ryder and the National Enterprise Board). More recently, the Conservative governments of 1979 onwards have drawn on the contribution of those who have run successful commercial operations before being asked to offer their advice and assistance to government and the public services (Rayner, Griffiths and Levene).

The link between commercial management and public services (broadly defined) has not been entirely one-way. Senior personnel, both political and official, have often on retirement become involved in trading concerns. Some significant management processes – operational research for example – have enjoyed the initial on most significant phase of their development in the public services, often at times of war. Joining the worlds of private management and public service has been a lengthy and continuing debate about the nature of the management process in both fields of activity. There are three main lines of argument. The first is that the nature of the management process is inherently similar, regardless of the activity toward which that process is directed. Perhaps unsurprisingly, the principal proponent of management as a 'scientific' and therefore universal process was a firm advocate of this view. As Taylor wrote earlier this century: 'The fundamental principles of scientific management are applicable to all kinds of human activities, from our simplest individual acts to the work of our greatest corporations' (Taylor, 1947, p. 4).

Other writers more recently have argued that there is a blurring of the differences between public and private. This is a more sophisticated development of the Taylor proposition that in many respects the procedures and processes employed to manage in the different spheres are similar where the nature of the decision to be made and the implementation of that decision is the same. This theme is supported by Allison (1983), who makes his point nicely in this title: 'Public and private management: are they fundamentally alike in all unimportant respects?' What seems clear, however, is that in many cases the manager in public services will not be able simply to apply techniques and processes held in common with the private sector, because of broader considerations which flow from the nature of public policy and decisions about that policy.

The argument that the management process in public and private sectors is completely different also has a long intellectual pedigree, and is supported by both detailed observation of practice in different organisations and by examination of the management experience of those who have worked in both sectors. In the next section of this chapter the specificity of managing local government is examined in more detail but there are elements of differentiation that run throughout the entire range of public services. Thus, for example, the concern for financial accountability is a common feature in all public services – often to a degree which is far beyond any material significance, and even though corrupt and fraudulent behaviour is not very prevalent in British public institutions. That emphasis on public accountability is also one element of the political environment within which all public services operate, regardless of any change in organisational form that is created. So, for example, private-sector managers involved in training and enterprise companies and local enterprise companies chafe against the bonds of financial accountability demanded by the National Audit Office.

Even successful managers from the private sector are sometimes unable to adjust to a political environment and the broader sense of public accountability which that requires. There are numerous examples of highly effective managers who have not successfully made that transition, as in the case of Sir Robert Reid who took over as Chairman of British Rail in 1990. A report assessing his performance one year later cited by one insider's comment: 'The jury is out on his competence, but people are starting to say, we will never find out, because his political skills are not good enough. He is not creating enough political space for himself to wield any influence' (Thomson, 1991, p. 19).

The emergence and use of the term 'Public Management' – or, as it is sometimes called, 'New Public Management' – is perhaps an inevitable reflection of an attempt to synthesise the two competing arguments of 'different' and inherently 'similar'. This interpretation of public-service management as a phenomenon distinct from both 'private management' and 'public administration' has seen a pronounced development in the latter part of the 1970s and throughout the 1980s. However, it is important to see this not just as a reordering of intellectual and academic categories but a reflection of some of the broader changes that are occurring within our society and those of other advanced industrial countries. One academic critic has observed that:

> There is no particular point in trying to draw fine distinctions between the various schools of thought here, especially since many of them are not themselves particularly precisely defined. What is worth noting, however, is, first, that their recent appearance, all over the western world, is almost certainly linked to deep changes in the environment for public agencies but, second, that we should not assume that the issues they address are entirely new (Gunn, p. 45, 1987).

Hood (1991) has outlined what he considered to be the main elements, or 'doctrinal components' of the 'new public management'. It is suggested that there are seven main elements that appear in one form or another in any examination of the changing organisation of public service delivery. Not all organisations will have necessarily experienced the introduction of these; not every part of large and multifunctional organisations, such as local authorities, have seen them all put in place for each part of the organisation. They will, however, be present in one form or another and to a greater or lesser degree in most of the public organisations that operate within the United Kingdom and other comparable OECD countries. The characteristics mentioned include: 'Hands-on professional management', often with a clearly defined account-ability for particular functions and actions within the organisation. In many local authorities now, for example, there is an increasing emphasis (in job description and job title) on the 'accountability' of particular managers, and their responsibility for a named range of tasks and responsibilities.

Two of the key characteristics of the new public management are closely linked – explicit standards and measures of performance, and an increased emphasis on output control. The former, it has been argued in the recent consultation documents from the Audit Commission (1992a) and the Local Authority Accounts Commission (1992), take the form of 'performance indicators' as essential features for judging the efficiency of a wide range of local authority services. The emphasis on output stresses a concern for results rather than an emphasis on process – an overconcentration on the latter is seen as a feature of degenerate and self-regarding bureaucracies whether in the public or private sector. The powerful observation that managers should be as concerned with 'doing the right thing' rather than just 'doing it right' serves to emphasise the degree to which in central and local government management processes in particular, the emphasis has often in the past been on the latter rather than on the former.

Another feature which is claimed to characterise the new approaches to public service management is the continuing disag-gregation of operational units in the public sector. In local autho-rities we have the imposition of competitive tendering and the creation of 'client' and 'contractor' functions in many local author-ity services. That process has both contributed to and been produced by another feature of the changing pattern of public service management – a shift towards ideas of competitive provision. The long-established expectation of public tendering for purchase of hard products – building, equipment, etc. – is now being supple-mented by a requirement for a competitive tendering for an array of services and activities.

Accompanying all of this has been, in many sectors and across many societies, a prescriptive argument for an increased emphasis on private sector styles of management. This is seen both in the broader rhetoric of being 'more businesslike' and also through an emphasis on particular management approaches and techniques – for example, an increased flexibility of staffing and pay and reward systems; a general emphasis on a 'leaner' form of management structure; and a recognition of a more competitive environment. In broad terms we see an increased emphasis in the management of the public services on the introduction of some methods and processes which are value-neutral and uncontroversial (e.g. improved investment appraisal) alongside those which are highly controversial and of disputed validity (e.g. performance-related pay). The impetus for much of this change has come from both the broader and changing environment in which local authorities operate and from prodding by such bodies as the Audit Commission. Released from the constraints of his role as director of that organisation, Howard Davies has been able to bluntly express his 'conviction that only by introducing more private company practices into public services will councils become responsive to their customers and avidly pursue efficiency and quality' (Davies, 1992, p. 12). Most significantly perhaps, and as an underlying element in all of the other management changes, has been the consistent and persistent pressure in many developed societies simply to reduce the cost of public service provision. This process, it is claimed, will ensure that public services are provided with a greater measure of cost discipline. Almost by definition, *good* managers are those people who will 'do more with less'.

It is important to distinguish one further feature that characterises the current pronounced emphasis on improved management in local government; a feature that is not touched upon by Hood or other writers. That further element is the extent to which, in recent years, the emphasis on improved management has permeated throughout the whole of local government. The major local government management reports of the 1960s and early 1970s all appeared to assume that 'management' was in some way the province of the most elite parts of an organisation. The implicit assumption in all of these documents is that a concern for management is sufficiently addressed if account is taken of the demands made on members, on the policy and resources committee in particular, and on the chief officers' management team. The more recent changes to be observed in the structure of local authorities show an increased emphasis on the management responsibilities of staff at the heart of the organisation. These are staff who would previously have seen their role defined purely in professional terms: a principal engineer, a senior architect, a senior social worker. Now the perception of their role within the organisation, and the way in which it is defined in their job title and description, unequivocally ascribes management functions and responsibilities to such a post. This of course has been a process characterised by considerable tension and difficulty in many cases. It is therefore appropriate to consider here whether managment in local government is in some way distinct and unique.

Managing in local government – is it different?

One thing that *is* now clearly different about managing in local government is that, from job titles alone, we can infer that far more people are expected to do it. From Renfrew District Council with its 'managing director' to Essex County with a 'corporate services manager' and Tower Hamlets with 'area managers' we see a real contrast with the days when managers ran only public baths, the works depot and the slaughterhouse.

It is also possible to observe that the one of the key enhanced responsibilities of the new managers is to turn the organisation outward rather than inward. The job descriptions for a newly reorganised cadre of social work managers in Lothian Region (1992) state that a principal day-to-day task is 'to promote a culture of responsiveness to changing consumer need and demand and the development of good standards of professional practice'. In a sense the emphasis on the 'management' task, as opposed to 'administration', marks a shift in local government assumptions which is parallell to the shift from *production* orientation to *marketing* orientation seen in manufacturing and trading concerns over the past fifty to sixty years. This shift from a concept of administration to one of management also reflects major differences in the way that the 'management' task is carried out in local government. If we are to see how (and whether) this is different from managing in the trading sector then we must look for these differences in three central elements of the management world:

(1) the environment;
(2) the links between the environment and the organisation;
(3) the internal structures and processes of the organisation.

The environment

The extent of market exposure

Local government organisations are predominantly financed by
predetermined appropriations rather than customer-driven earnings. A library that suffers a slump in borrowers is insulated from
a requirement for immediate remedial action, so both local library
staff and the local service manager can defer action on that loss of
demand for often considerable periods of time. Trading companies
must respond quickly to the demands of a volatile marketplace.
Conversely, increased demand for services within the wide portfolio
of activities and services for which councils are responsible is
frequently met with demand-squeezing behaviours, rationing and
'customer shedding', rather than a transfer of resources. In many
authorities the service and budgetary assumption was for many
years that long-established services should continue; new initiatives
were either not developed or were subject of intense and prolonged
argument over support and resources. In a climate of this type there
is constantly a temptation for the operational manager to seek to
limit demand for services rather than to respond flexibly and
creatively to demand and need for services within the community.

The legislative base

Many council services and activities are predetermined by a
statutory base which requires that certain things be done or
provides that other things are not done. Whilst legislation provides
the framework for local government services – and is indeed a
precondition for the existence of the local authority – it often creates
a climate of constraint which many feel they cannot step outside.
There is often the tendency to overstate the degree of constraint and
restraint which legislation imposes. It is also clear that areas of local
government activity have been developed through the creativity and

innovative approach of councillors and staff who have pushed against the boundaries of legislative control. Thirty years ago very few local authorities had any interest in economic development and the creation of employment, now it is commonplace to find it viewed as an activity central to their role within the community, and council activities are planned accordingly.

The demands of financial accountability

Because local authorities are public bodies, funded principally through public taxation, there is an expectation of greater standards of public financial accountability than might be sought in other organisations. In some cases this can lead to an excessive formalisation and control of budgetary and spending decisions. Rigorous checking, rather than approximation is often seen as essential to the monitoring of operations. A comparison can be made with market- and profit-led organisations, where considerations of financial 'materiality' suggest that other procedures would be better employed. So, for example, many of the financial mechanisms of the typical local authority are geared toward financial accounting rather than financial management. It may seem on occasion that the principal consideration is completion of the final accounts at the end of the financial year, rather than the construction of management information systems that aid operational managers in their decision-making and spending.

Values and public choice

Local authorities are democratically elected, and members are accountable to the communities which they represent. There are many interests at play within those communities, and this can frequently produce a variety of – often competing – external demands and influences upon the organisation. The key role for the politician, and often for senior staff as well, is to handle the bargaining and brokerage process which is necessary to ensure that those competing demands are reconciled in a way that enables the organisation to achieve a broad range of community objectives. That is very rarely easy, and it is made even more difficult in

circumstances when the council as a whole, or individual representatives of the authority, are not willing to acknowledge publicly that
there may be competing interests, not all of which can be met. In
fact, some of the most imaginative developments seen in the local
authority housing field in recent years have taken place in those
authorities in which there have been initiatives involving discussion
with residents and tenants about the way in which different demands
are reconciled and the degree to which the council is or is not able to
meet some of those demands.

A complex environment

For any manager operating within the public services, the complexity of the environment is much greater than is found in even the
most sophisticated of trading operations.

Perhaps the factor most characteristic of the environment in
which managers and local government must work is that the
potential demands that can be placed on the 'public domain' are
literally unbounded. There is an expectation that government, and
local government, will respond to any legitimate and socially
acceptable demands voiced by individuals or communities. This
may be in the context of market failure (perhaps a shop failing in
a remote community) or natural disaster (a river floods, crops fail),
or even terrorist action (the Lockerbie disaster). In any event, there
is an assumption – frequently not expressed until the untoward
event occurs – that 'they . . . will do something about it'.

The link between the organisation and the environment

Limited market signals

Concepts such as sale, price and profit are terms which are not used
in, or even relevant to, many of the functions and services for which
local authorities assume a responsibility. Consequently, until recently few local authorities employed the relevant management
techniques which helped to set these market signals in context. In
recent years, increasing numbers of councils have been developing a
more sophisticated approach to this process. Nonetheless, pricing

strategies are often ill-informed, arbitrary and related to historic practice rather than any conscious strategy. This is particularly pronounced in those services which are perceived as being related to 'need', even when (as much research shows) the actual distribution of services is not based on real need or is redistributive in nature. So, for example, any study of the take-up of home-care services through social workers or social services departments will probably show that services are often not allocated to those in greatest need but simply to those who are equipped to secure access to the services, because they are better informed, more articulate, etc.

In many cases councils are reluctant to come to terms with the principles and implications of charging for services, even when they are discretionary and alternative providers are in evidence. So it is only in recent years that local authorities have begun to experiment with off-peak pricing and variable pricing strategies for sports and leisure facilities. The sometimes capricious and unconsidered basis of pricing decisions can be seen across councils controlled by all political parties, and reflects an historic reluctance to think rigorously about this aspect of the management process.

Resource allocation

The provision of council resources is generally demand-led, though often in a crude way, and still rationed. It is rare to find even rudimentary attempts to assess potential return, even in quasi-market settings such as the provision of workspace buildings. Change is occurring in this field, particularly in capital investment, but in many authorities discretionary investment decisions are still on occasion made on the most uncertain and sometimes whimsical of grounds.

The power of force

Government, even local government, has unique powers of coercion generally not available to private trading concerns. A planner or a road engineer can negotiate for land purchase knowing that at the conclusion of the process there will, if necessary, be a compulsory purchase order rather than frustration. It is rare for such an overriding power to be made explicit to the public, but for many senior staff, particularly in regulatory activities, it is an implicit element in the relationship with the consumer of local government services.

Extensive expectations

Citizens and communities will often have high expectations of the scope of provision available from council services. This phenomenon is often most pronounced in areas of predominantly local authority housing ownership where virtually all public and social activity is influenced by council ownership of facilities and provision of services. In such housing estates the council is expected not simply to provide appropriate and well-maintained housing in exchange for rent, but to monitor and police the behaviour of those tenants whose lifestyle and actions are not considered acceptable to their neighbours. The council will also, in some cases, be expected to support and sustain local shopping provision – even when many residents generally choose to do their shopping elsewhere, and thus contribute to the decline of those shops.

Working in the goldfish bowl

For anyone working in the public services, public scrutiny is more extensive than would be the case in the normal operation of any trading concern. There is an expectation – certainly in the United Kingdom – not simply of high standards of performance, but of probity and a high standard of public behaviour. In effect there are two separate considerations here. We have a general expectation that public agencies will operate procedures that in an even-handed and transparent fashion – we would not expect that in a car showroom. In addition to that there is the expectation that public officials and elected members will behave with appropriate standards of propriety in relation to purchasing, expenditure, and appointment. The publicity given to those rare cases where this does not occur is indicative of the degree to which this is taken for granted in our society.

The fourth 'E'

The drive for economy, efficiency, and effectiveness, characterised the thrust of public management thinking during the 1980s. It often seemed as though the fourth E – 'equity' – had been forgotten. There appeared to be a growing perception of public service users as 'customers', with the implicit assumption that they could either take or leave the services on offer – as they would do in a shop. This perhaps neglected the consideration that a public service is one in which people are dealt with consistently, in a comparable fashion in comparable cases, and one which takes account of the extent to which other organisations may have failed to provide for people. Put simply, people expect to be treated 'fairly' by public agencies.

It is frequently difficult to balance this wish for fairness against the clear framework of procedures and prescribed solutions which are created in order to ensure the consistency which is also sought in public organisations. This difficulty of balance, coupled with the limitations on delegation within public organisations, causes that frequent frustration that people feel when they see a sensible, commonsense solution denied to them because the organisation and the people within it are required to go through certain procedures and to adhere to fixed routines. One further complication for the manager in the local authority is that such a perspective is always expressed from the point of view of the subject of any action. If that same person were the observer of an action with no particular personal interest, their equally common sense view might well be 'Why don't they stick to the procedures?'

Complex objectives

That one person may have more than one perspective of the way in which the local authority operates, even mutually contradictory perspectives, is illustrative of the extent to which all councils operate within the context of a multiplicity of complex, competing and perhaps even irreconcilable objectives. One person, or a group of people, may wish to see the council effecting a change in their environment which is impossible to achieve without impinging on their own capacity to act. For example, as a resident in an edge-of-centre street they may wish to see street parking controlled, but not be willing to pay the parking charges which are a usual corollary of most forms of parking regulation. As though it were not enough for one individual or group of individuals to inflict a complex array of demands on the organisation, that process is infinitely multiplied, so that local authorities – as so many other large and particularly public organisations – have a multiplicity of 'stake holders', all of whom are making demands upon them. This complexity of objectives will invariably lead to uncertainty for those at the centre of policy decisions, and those responsible for implementation. When we add to this the difficulty of determining criteria for successful achievement – a characteristic feature of many public organisations – then the demands upon the manager become substantial, highly frustrating, and often unacheivable.

The structures and processes of the organisation

Probity and consistency versus innovation

Traditions of public service and public management in Britain emphasise probity and integrity in personal behaviour, along with consistency of practice. The first two qualities are both understandable and desirable; the latter can too easily ossify into rigidity and resistance to change. Innovation implies risk, and there is much in the culture of British public services which has for a long time militated against risk-taking. Staff are rewarded for 'not getting it wrong' as opposed to 'getting it right'. Innovation occurs, but it does so in an often patchy and unrecognised fashion. One of the most interesting features observable in British local government is the very ad hoc and ill-planned way in which good practice – and the lessons of unsuccessful innovation – are disseminated throughout the different local authorities. When urged to speak out and publicise their successful innovation, practitioners will often express a modest disclaimer that 'it's nothing really'. There is something in the pressure to consistency and equity that can too often create a quiet uniformity and an unwillingness to be seen to break ranks, either at organisational or individual level.

Unclear performance goals

When asked by government to do so, the Audit Commission and the Local Authority Accounts Commission have found it difficult to define rigorous and helpful means of assessing good performance for different local government services. This in itself is a reflection of the degree to which it is exceptionally difficult to define effective performance goals for many public services and free goods. In many cases this may be a reflection of the uncertainties attached to the boundaries of our different social institutions and the multiplicity of demands we place upon them. It is, by any reckoning, difficult to provide an effective housing service in many of our large urban areas. The demands placed upon the organisation for accommodation, the shortfall in resources and the changing and unstable population mean that there is often an excess of demand over acceptable supply. Being a landlord is difficult enough – over and above that requirement, many housing departments are then expected to operate as a surrogate social work department cum mediation/counselling service. Similarly, social work or social services departments in many councils often find their staff acting as a substitute for the Benefits Agency. Whether negotiating, mediating, or in some cases actually paying out cash, the diversion of energies from the main tasks of the organisation does not contribute to effective performance.

Performance uncertainties make delegation difficult

As many large and successful organisations have demonstrated, the clearest and simplest means of delegating authority is to do so on a financial basis. There are limits to expenditure, there is an expectation of return, there is a programme for investment, and there are corporate policies and procedures – within those parameters the manager is allowed to get on with it. In local government it is not that easy. If it is possible to make performance criteria more explicit – a process which will emerge from the discussion about how more effectively to measure performance – then it will become easier. It will still be a debatable area, since the variety of actors who legitimately have an interest in the decision-making process (officers, members, committees, partner organisations) may all in effect wish to limit the delegated authority available to any given member of staff. With the continuing requirements for equity and consistency but the developing drive for flexibility within local authorities, effective delegation will become a very central test of how well the organisation is growing and changing.

Discipline versus reward

In many public agencies, as in local authorities, both sanction and reward systems are structured in a way that minimises the relationship between manager and staff. Recruitment is frequently through a panel appointment, and in some cases the accountable manager has no involvement in the recruitment process. At best he or she will be party to a decision made collectively; in some cases the other parties to the decision have no responsibility for the performance outcome of the appointment. Where appraisal schemes are in place they are often structured on the basis that the appraiser is not in a position to provide any form of reward package (not necessarily financial) to the person who has performed effectively – or, for that matter, to take action against those who have not performed effectively. In some authorities the different elements of the employment relationship are so discrete that an appraisal system can exist alongside a recruitment and promotion system which does not acknowledge that there is any formal process of appraisal within the council.

Conversely, the disciplinary process in all local authorities is invariably subject to internal and external checks beyond the statutory procedures. This may be a desirable element in local authorities' desire to be seen as good employers, but it does nonetheless create one more barrier between manager and staff in a matter which is central to the working relationship. The previously mentioned requirement for consistency of practice in the operation of the authority, along with the difficulties of dealing with a multiplicity of professional and occupational groups and a complex negotiating mechanism, has led to a complicated and over-prescriptive 'grade maze'. This invariably places considerable pressure upon the mechanisms available for encouraging motivation and flexibility within the organisation.

How staff are motivated

The motivation of staff is discussed in greater detail in a later chapter but it is perhaps relevant to note here that local authorities have features in common with other large organisations, as well as features which distinguish them from these. They share with many large organisations the common tendency to cap expectation and performance within all grades of staff but particularly amongst those at managerial and professional level. The limitations of a hierarchical structure, the procedures and mechanisms that seek to create consistency of practice, and limitations on the capacity to delegate, all serve to suppress the talent and performance of employees within the organisation.

Until recently one thing which did distinguish local government from many other large trading organisations was the highly prescriptive and rigid formulae employed to determine salary. National agreements were not simply a base from which an authority might determine appropriate pay levels but a prescription from the centre to be applied under all circumstances. In times of pay restraint they were viewed as being, in effect, legally prescriptive.

Securing staff commitment

Securing staff commitment is suggested as a goal – though perhaps more often a chimera – which all managers are urged to strive for, certainly in the more evangelical management publications. Different local authorities have pursued many different methods to try and achieve this apparently desirable goal. For reasons which are not clear, there does seem to be a distinction between the private and the public in this very significant area. Very few local authorities report achieving the apparent degree of motivation and commitment that some – albeit not many – large private companies achieve.

Subsequent chapters will explore in more detail the degree to which the distinctions suggested above between managing in local government and managing elsewhere actually have an impact on the way in which organisations are run.

A cross-party view?

As the article cited at the beginning of this chapter argues, the agenda set by this government has taken a particular form, and has emphasised those elements of the managerial revolution which find their greatest appeal amongst the new right in party politics.

Increased competition, privatisation where possible, enforced tendering, disaggregation of large multifunctional service organisations and the individualisation of reward packages for public service staff, are part of the armoury of approaches which the new right in many countries has employed as part of the effort to reshape the public sector.

However, the emphasis on improved efficiency and effectiveness in the public sector is solely confined to the Conservative Party. The Liberal Democrats have consistently argued for enhanced mechanisms of management efficiency in public services generally, and in local government in particular. They were for a long time enthusiastic advocates of 'performance review' in local government, and in some councils such mechanisms for review were established on their initiative. Indeed, in some councils where there was no majority, the introduction of such changes was a critical factor in the Liberal Democrats' support for the administration. A party publication on local government reform (1991) argues that one of the key principles for local government change is that: 'internal and external mechanisms must be put in place to ensure councils provide services efficiently and cost-effectively'.

Within the Labour Party the emphasis on enhanced effectiveness in public services is most pronounced in policy documents, such as the Labour Party's response to the Citizen's Charter. This has a key passage which argues:

> As a nation we have a poor history of investing in management development and expertise. We too often promote able people to management positions and expect them intuitively to know how to manage people and complex processes. Better training for managers is essential, we will pay particular attention to management practice in the public sector. The public and private sectors share a number of common features. But the art of managing public services also demands different skills and perspectives.

More directly, Neil Kinnock, then leader of the Labour Party, made his position on public services clear in the period immediately before the 1992 election: 'There is no question of spending more than the nation can afford and that will continue throughout a Labour Government. Provision will depend on performance' (*The Times*, 1 February 1992). So the Labour Party can be seen as differentiating between the public services and private industry, but arguing forcefully that effective management is important for effective public services. That position has emerged as part of a lively and continuing debate within the Labour Party.

Summary

This chapter has attempted to argue that the shift towards an emphasis on enhanced managerial practice in the public services in general, and in local government in particular, is not a fashion or a fad. It is a long-term secular trend that will continue as part of the policy armoury of politicians from all the major parties. Such practice will therefore have to become embedded in the practice of politicians and managers in local authorities throughout the United Kingdom. The next chapter reviews some of the major changes in the environment of local government that has lead to this position.

Some points for discussion

1. Why do you think there has been an increasing emphasis on the effective management of the public services in recent years?
2. Has this change affected you, whether you work in local government or use services provided by local government?
3. Is 'effective management' the most important aspect of effective public services?
4. What could private management learn from public management?
5. Could local government find other ways to improve the quality of public services?

2 Local Government: Developments and Trends

The previous chapter argued that the increasing interest in how local government is 'managed' is not a passing phenomenon, and that the interest will continue to grow and extend its influence across all local authorities, with considerable implications for all who are involved in any way. This concern for more effective management is not the prerogative of one particular party, or of any particular group of individuals within local government; nor is it solely a contrived and artificial theme for academic commentators to pursue. The effective management of local government is now of interest to all those who are elected to serve, those who work for, and those who have facilities and services provided by the local authority.

This interest in how local government is run does indeed represent a change from the observation we might have made fifty, forty, thirty or even twenty years ago. We do not have to look for the absurdities of a British *Clochemerle* to accept that for many years local government was seen as – and was – something of a backwater. Even during those periods when considerable and sustained growth in local government expenditure and functions was under-way, there was a recognition that those organisations responsible for the growth of much of the postwar welfare state were not particularly well equipped to handle the task. The post Second World War expansion of public services demonstrated central government's reluctance to entrust responsibilities to the local authorities. Bevan, as the relevant minister, had considerable difficulty in securing a key role for councils in housing development, and their involvement in the development of the health service was severely curtailed. A subsequent (Conservative) minister expressed his doubts about the capacity of local government to meet the demands that expanding social programmes placed upon it. 'It would be laughable to maintain that every bit of the present local government structure, mostly dating from 60 to 70 years ago, is effective and convenient for present day needs. I have no prejudices or preconceptions myself. My one concern is that we shall end up with a local government system that is effective and convenient for present day needs', was the public observation of the then government minister, Henry Brooke, in 1960 (Benham, 1964, p. 14).

The interest of the reformers was invariably focused on boundaries and structure, rather than on the way in which councils were managed and run; the tension between those two approaches has been extensively discussed in various books. Even in such studies, the shape and form of local government attracts far more attention than the manner in which those reshaped institutions might be run, with Brand (1974) affording one paragraph of his detailed study of reorganisation to the reports concerned respectively with staffing and management of local government in England and Wales.

The main theme of this book is the way in which local authorities are managed, rather than the manner in which they are structured and the boundaries that confine them. At a time when the shape of local government throughout Great Britain was giving concern to those at the centre of the policy community – the 1950s and 1960s – the reality inside many local authorities was frustratingly oppressive for many who worked there. This was delightfully captured in a contemporary novel, *Room at the Top*, the main theme of which was about the ambition of one bright young person to escape from the Town Hall:

Even now, I don't like to remember the Efficient Zombie. . . . Working under him was always a strain. . . . We were expected to work all the time, which appears reasonable enough. The drawback was that we were always beginning jobs and then being forced to break them off which in the long run wastes more time than the odd ten minutes spent smoking or flirting. . . . Had his staff been allowed to establish their own rhythm of working it wouldn't have been necessary (Braine, 1989, p. 43).

Some local authorities still have individuals within their ranks those who resemble the Efficient Zombie. The significant change in many authorities is that a different approach to management is now being encouraged, in a conscious effort to effect a change of practice based on cultural change rather than simple prescription.

The reasons for change

A different approach to managing in local government and a concern about the way in which local government is managed has emerged over the past twenty to twenty-five years. One of the most significant reasons has been the pressure on resources and the constraints of a far stricter financial regime, and this is the first major change factor which is discussed more fully below. There are however numerous reasons over and above that financial squeeze; they range from a changing – and moving – population to a changing perception of what is considered socially desirable. Such changes have, often in a complex and interrelated fashion, created as significant a pressure for change as has the strict financial regime. However it is first appropriate to consider whether local government has a long-term future, since some commentators have implied that the recent experience of local government suggests just the opposite.

Local government – an institution in decline?

The period prior to the Second World War has been described as 'the heyday of local government' (Stevenson, 1984). Over that lengthy period in the first half of this century, major municipal functions and initiatives were developed in councils of every kind. Herbert Morrison, as leader of the London County Council, had such powers and resources at his disposal that he was able to defy central government and build a new Waterloo bridge, despite government disapproval. In Kirkintilloch, a small town outside Glasgow, the future secretary of state for Scotland established a municipal cinema and bank, and bulk-bought respectable suits for local men.

In a passage which uses the device of repetition to emphasise the importance of local government in the life of the community, Sidney Webb highlighted the way in which a councillor could progress through the town and:

> walk along the municipal pavement, lit by the municipal gas and cleansed by municipal brooms with the municipal water, and seeing by the municipal clock in the municipal marketplace that he is too early to meet his children coming from the municipal

school hard by the county lunatic asylum and municipal hospital, will use the national telegraph system to tell them not to walk through the municipal park but to come by the municipal tram to meet him in the municipal reading room by the municipal art gallery, museum and library (quoted in Fraser, 1979, p. 171).

In sad contrast to this paean to the achievements of collective and governmental provision, some authors have suggested that the entire period after the Second World War has been one of continuous and long term decline for both Webb-inspired collectivist civic values and, in practical terms for the functions and status of local government. There is some dispute about the time-frame of this alleged decline, with some opting for the period after the War and others suggesting that 1930–1974 is a 'period of decline' (Byrne, 1986). The principal features characterising that decline are often suggested as being a loss of basic functions (gas and electricity); a failure to gain new functions (New Towns and control of motorway developments); a loss of financial independence (increased reliance on externally controlled funding); and increased central control (most recently, council tax capping). Stoker (1991) has suggested that this rather gloomy analysis is oversimplified, in that whilst local government has been affected by this process, the repeated attempts by central government to control local authorities have often been less successful than the initiators might have hoped.

To take a longer term perspective, it seems reasonable to observe that as citizens and consumers of local services we have expected local government to do more, and to do different things. We have often seen this expressed through parliament legislation the Environmental Protection Act of 1990, for example and direction by government County Structure Planning in England and Wales. Simultaneously we have perhaps not been fully ready to recognise that .the changes we implicitly and explicitly demand of local authorities in terms of the service and facilities they provide requires changes in those organisations; in their funding, in their powers and in the manner in which they are organised and managed. Travers (1986, p. xi) has summarised this in relation to the financing of local government:

It would be wrong to see the present crisis in the relationship between local and central government as something sudden and

unexpected. . . . Governments have regularly restated the importance of healthy local democracy without taking steps to ensure
its preservation. . . . Since the start of the 20th century Parliament
has vastly increased its demand for services provided by local
government, despite recent transfers of some provision to central
government and its agencies. . . Local authorities have had to
expand their provision without access to a single new tax.

Nonetheless, those increasing expectations – of government and
society – have seen local government current expenditure continue
to increase as a proportion of gross domestic product between 1950
and the 1980s – the term of that period of alleged 'decline' – as
Figure 2.1 indicates.

At a local level, a town as small as Colchester was building the
equivalent of one house per day in the period immediately following
the Second World War and throughout the 1950s and 1960s,
Birmingham was building up to 6,000 council houses a year. In

**FIGURE 2.1   Local expenditure as percentage of GDP, United
Kingdom, 1950–81**

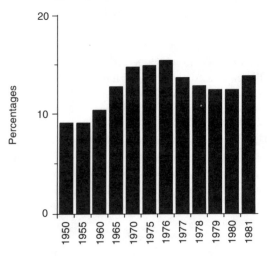

Sources: Newton and Karran (1985); Central Statistical Office (1993).

that period local government had become 'big government . . . and big business' (Kingdom, 1991, p. 1). Even now, although the shape of spending and resource patterns has changed, expenditure on local government in the UK is now approximately 10 per cent of gross domestic product. In Scotland almost half of the monies allocated each year to those budget heads controlled by the Scottish Office are immediately allocated on to local authorities, as Table 2.1 shows.

TABLE 2.1 **Total public expenditure controlled by the Scottish Office and amount allocated to local government expenditure (£1000M)**

Year	Total SO expenditure	Local government expenditure	%
1987–88	7858	3964	50.4
1988–89	8512	4314	50.6
1989–90	8972	4621	51.5
1990–91	9690	4811	49.6
1991–92*	11733	5786	49.3

*estimate.
Sources: The Scottish Office (1993); The Government's Expenditure Plans 1993/4–1995/6, Cmnd 2214 (London: HMSO)

It is also apparent that discussion about local government as part of the broader political debate has moved from 'a constitutional fringe show [to become] one of the most important theatres of British politics' (Kingdom, 1991, p. 1) Directly or indirectly, local government has been responsible for the removal from office of two recent prime ministers.

Local government is still a significant and vital institution in the framework of our society. It does still provide a range of services and facilities which support us literally from cradle to grave. Our births, and those of our children, are registered with a local authority officer; if we die without means or relatives our local council will bury us and seek to trace any relatives. In the next section of this chapter what is discussed is that complex array of features which has led us to a greater concern with the way in which those institutions of local government are managed.

Raising and spending money

As indicated above, the level of expenditure on local government
services is now at a higher level as a proportion of GDP than it was
even in the periods of most rapid growth during the mid 1960s.
Historically, both increasing and attempting to confine local
authority expenditure – often as a sharp reversal of previous policy
– have not been a prerogative of any one particular party of
government. In 1932 (under an essentially Conservative government), aggregate annual expenditure by local authorities reached a
level of just under 13 per cent of gross domestic product, a
proportion it did not reach again until 1975 (Labour government)
– the high-point of the postwar period.

Whilst the long-term trend has been an increase in the overall level
of expenditure incurred by local government there have of course
been dramatic changes within relatively short periods. The most
substantial and sharp reduction in recent years was in the mid 1970s
when the then Secretary of State for the Environment, Anthony
Crosland, issued a circular to local authorities calling for a
'standstill' on local authority expenditure in the 1975/76 financial
year. That standstill actually became a reduction, in terms of the
proportion of gross domestic product, and it was achieved through
dramatic reductions in capital expenditure with a limited impact on
current expenditure. This concentration on saving current expenditure at the cost of capital was clearly acceptable – if not welcomed –
by those who were involved in that decision-making process at both
central and local government level. The net impact, of course, was to
export the impact of such expenditure restraint into a diverse and
not well organised sector of the economy – building contractors and
materials suppliers – rather than the better organised (politically and
industrially) local authorities. The squeeze in resources and the
implications for local government services has been discussed
extensively elsewhere. The perceived impact and consequences of
this will inevitably depend on the political perspective of those
people involved.

Two former Cabinet Ministers indicate in their very different
ways how they have viewed that process. Barbara Castle, in the mid
1970s Secretary of State for Social Services, was both participant
and observer in the process of determining local authority expenditure: 'There had been an outcry against the so called "standstill" on

local authority expenditure next year, which the councils unanimously denounced as meaning savage cuts. . . . It just is not on. Checks on growth and expenditure are one thing, and painful enough, but actual cuts, as far as I am concerned, are out' (Castle, 1980, p. 531). The perspective from the right, in the eyes of Nicholas Ridley, is dramatically different: 'I discovered the meaning of the word "cuts" in a conversation with some left-wing teachers from my constituency who used the phrase as a sort of war cry . . . their sheer zeal persuaded them, and much of the media, that there really were savage cuts in all the social programmes' (Ridley, 1992, p. 64).

Whether we take the view of Castle or Ridley, the pattern of both external and internal financing for local government has been consistent for almost twenty years now. The level of growth in government preferred expenditure has consistently been exceeded by actual expenditure – though even so, that actual expenditure has often not been at a rate that matched inherited commitments or desired local government-policy initiatives. The moves initiated by Crosland during the discussion about IMF support for the pound in the mid-1970s led to an exhortation to local authorities to keep their expenditure levels down, or if possible to reduce them. This was followed by direct action by the Labour government to reduce the amount of external support made available to local authorities through the then Rate Support Grant. Figure 2.2 shows the trend during this period and into the 1980s.

The election of the first Conservative government led by Mrs Thatcher saw a continuing reduction in central government support for local government services. This was coupled at first with further exhortation, and subsequently with compulsory measures, to limit the amount of money local authorities could raise locally through the rates – whether household or business – and reduce in the amount of money they could spend – regardless of its source. This process is described elsewhere both for England and Wales and for Scotland (Travers, 1986; Midwinter, 1987). The consequence of this financial pressure varied from council to council, and within individual councils over time and depending on circumstance. Some councils accepted – and even welcomed – government urging to cut expenditure and reduce the demand on domestic and commercial ratepayers. Major management changes developed in response to this tighter financial climate; Cambridgeshire County Council, for

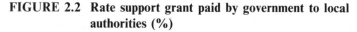

**FIGURE 2.2   Rate support grant paid by government to local
authorities (%)**

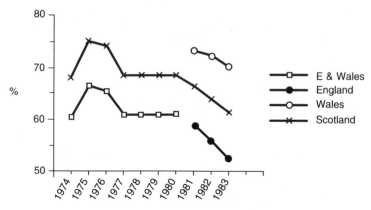

Sources: 'Rate Support Grant' 1983; London: 1983 mimeo Joint Local
Authority Associations.

example, introduced 'performance management' initially because of
limitations on expenditure. Other councils at first responded in the
traditional 'municipal meanness' fashion – closing public conve-
niences, limiting library hours and so on. Subsequently there was
recognition that in the longer term this was not an adequate
response and it was necessary to review the overall strategy of the
organisation. Arun District Council 'has adopted a strategic
management approach to its affairs since 1983'. It contrasts the
attitude in 1982 'a siege/inward attitude and nil rate growth priority'
with 1987 and 'a breakout/involvement attitude and measured rate
growth/spend up to and slightly over authorised level' (Local
Government Training Board, 1988). Other councils pursued a
course of resistance; publicly arguing against government policy,
campaigning to change government policy and at least initially
simply refusing to accept financial restraints. In some cases (such
as Liverpool) those policies appeared to be built around defiance to
collision point, though the underlying rationale for and consequences of that approach continue to be fiercely disputed.

Many councils have combined accommodation or defiance with a
process that might be best characterised as an attempt at evasion or

avoidance. Council finance officials have, during the 1980s and early 1990s, developed sophisticated and complex means of attempting to generate more and alternative sources of finance for the council, often popularly referred to as 'creative accounting'. This phrase, with its implication of rather shady behaviour, has served as a shorthand to encompass a variety of mechanisms, some relatively commonplace (more effective treasury management); others of a more bizarre nature (the sale and lease back of revenue-generating assets such as parking meters). Indeed, many councils have only exploited the opportunities made available through national and international financial deregulation in much the same way as many of their residents acquired new endowment mortgages to replace the repayment mortgage and used a little of the available surplus to buy a family holiday. The extent of that process can be seen in different parts of the country, where many of even the smallest and most conservative of councils have some form of 'covenant' finance in place. In any event, such relatively new financial instruments have demonstrated and tested the creativity of council finance officers in a way that has shown local authority officials to be fully as imaginative and flexible as their counterparts in the private sector, although sometimes in a manner which has caused concern to the regulatory bodies as well as some secretaries of state.

It is not intended to discuss the detail of local government finance here. It is important to stress the point that, particularly because of the mechanisms for external financial support through central government, some local authorities both in England and Wales and in Scotland have found in past years that their individual financial position is significantly different (for better or worse) than that of the generality of local authorities or the overall trend in central support to local government. One example of the way in which that level of central support varies between councils can be seen by comparing the figures for the Scottish regional councils as Figure 2.3 does.

If it is possible to generalise, it is reasonable to suggest that until the early part of the 1990s many local authorities were in their overall trend of available financial resources closer to the Castle perception of 'restraint' than the Ridley anticipation of 'cuts'. What we can also see emerging in the mid to late 1980s is a general reaction amongst many local authorities against the 1970s method of meeting financial restraint by simply not initiating or countenan-

FIGURE 2.3   Revenue expenditure supported by grant, 1991/2 (%)

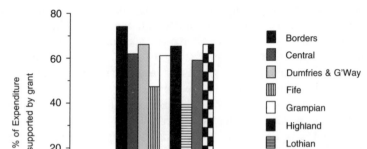

Source: Annual Reports of Regional Councils for relevant years.

cing any new developments within the organisation. The strategic shift, therefore, has been to a position of recognising financial restraint, and therefore reviewing and evaluating all of what the local authority does, rather than simply rejecting ideas for new growth and new development. Arun is one example; there are countless others in authorities of all sizes and controlled by different political parties.

In summary, a change in financial regime for local government has caused local authorities to protest, to retreat, and – in most cases – ultimately to adapt. Some have done so more successfully than others. The next section of this chapter considers some of the other factors which have required and caused local authorities to make that adaptation.

Some other influences on local government

An end of consensus?

Fierce political debate has long been a feature of elected local government in many parts of Great Britain – despite the popular inclination to wistfully recall otherwise. Local authorities are democratically elected institutions – the only ones outside parliament – and candidates stand for election on a political platform, whether or not that platform is overtly labelled with the name of a party. There is considerable evidence to show that the historical myth of non-party local government is just a myth in many parts of Great Britain. Nonetheless, there is equally evidence to suggest that in the period from the late 1970s onward, political organisation in local government became more widespread, partisanship became more emphatic and there has been increasingly pronounced and often fierce division between the party in control of a local authority and the party or parties in opposition. One consequence of this process, although other factors such as legislative change have been significant, is that established patterns of behaviour and organisation increasingly came under examination and challenge.

In the 1950s and early 1960s resort towns on the southern coasts of England with an overwhelming Conservative majority operated and managed municipal theatres, leisure facilities, even ice cream and catering operations. There was no assumption that the council should seek private tenders or franchises for those kind of activities – after all, all parties agreed that those facilities were significant features of the town and it was only sensible and right that the council should be responsible for them and run them directly. Similarly, in large towns and cities direct works organisations built and maintained local authority properties. Occasionally the efficiency and cost of those organisations would be the subject of dispute and disagreement. In some authorities a change of control from Labour to Conservative would see their existence challenged, or their size and scale reduced, but even those who would be assumed to favour the interests of the private sector over public services would often accept their continued presence. In councils where political partisanship was a long-established feature, some offices – and particularly in English authorities the mayoralty – would be allocated to members of minority parties without debate or serious discussion among the majority. In some of the smaller and less prominent councils, committee chairs would be shared between the parties, though rarely on anything resembling a proportional basis.

The experience of the 1980s has seen much of that habitual pattern of behaviour increasingly challenged and changed. Change of control in a council, particularly where there has been a pronounced and fierce level of partisanship, as between Labour and Conservative parties, can initiate major changes in the way in which the authority is run, and even produce the council's withdrawal from some services and facilities previously provided. This has been most obvious in those activities which have proved to be the bête noire of Conservative politicians at local and national level: equal opportunities initiatives; women's committees; programmes of positive action in favour of disadvantaged communities. However, over and above such clearly declaratory actions a change of political control is now increasingly likely to see councils reevaluating the entire range of activities and functions in which the authority is involved, and either seeking to re-order them or to manage them in a very different way. The experiences in Bradford, Brent and Ealing in the early 1990s are characteristic of this phenomenon.

Legislative change

Although we are not yet in a position to evaluate the full impact of the government's enforced legislation requiring local authorities to test certain services through 'competitive tendering', it seems clear that in many respects the organisational consequences of that legislation have perhaps had the greatest impact on local authorities of any of the other changes that have occurred during the 1980s. Prior to the provisions of the 1988 Act came into force, local authorities had a core of expertise accustomed to carrying out construction- and land-based activities. Until the practical implications of that Act became clear, very few authorities had even considered the possibility that there might be alternative non-council providers for services, functions and activities which they had simply assumed to be provided by the council through a directly employed workforce. The corollary is of course also true: until this time there were few companies involved in street cleansing and refuse collection, and building cleaning was a fragmented and rather marginal industry.

The impact of that legislation cannot be overestimated. In some cases, councils were forced to review activities which had escaped scrutiny for perhaps thirty or forty years. In every case, even where the direct labour or direct service organisation did not loose a tendered contract, the changes within that organisation and within related parts of the local authority have been dramatic and continuing in their impact.

Different ways of working

The requirement to face up to competitive tendering often led local authorities to make major changes in both organisational structure and working practice. This led to an increasing interest in the productivity of staff within the organisation, and indeed many local authorities have claimed major productivity improvements - particularly in those services provided by 'manual' workers.

Increasingly, local authority managers – and members – will be looking for similar improvements in productivity among staff employed in APT & C grades, among teachers, and among the uniformed emergency services. They will do so partly because of a visceral political reaction to some of the changes enforced through competitive tendering legislation. Many members clearly feel strongly that the burden of such changes has to date been borne by manual workers, who tend to be among the lowest paid local government staff, and the impact has not yet been felt by those employed in what are perceived as being secure and better paid positions among white-collar staff. They will also have an expectation that, if they wish to see services improved (the reason many members sought election), such improvement can now only be achieved through reordering the way in which services are delivered, rather than spending more money on increasing the number of staff providing those services. One chief executive in a Scottish District has described (Labour) members elected in the 1992 elections as 'more management minded . . . looking for value for money and keen to pursue their policies not just go along [with inherited programmes]' (Kerley, 1993, p. 22).

This phenomenon is not confined to local government or the public services. Both in this country and overseas there is increasing evidence to suggest that many large organisations providing services are looking very vigorously at the productivity of their white-collar and management staff. Recent changes in many service activities on both sides of the Atlantic suggests that many organisations are now addressing this aspect of service performance. Employers in different sectors are increasingly attempting to focus on white-collar productivity, and the consequences are being seen – or are projected to be seen – in various industries and services, as restructuring continues apace. A concern for white-collar productivity is also partly fuelled by another significant factor which will have an impact on the way in which local authority services are managed and delivered: demographic change.

The changing population

'The demographic time-bomb' is a term that has increasingly come to seem like a cliché in public policy discussion in the 1980s and early 1990s. The use of the metaphor 'time bomb' was presumably intended by those who coined it to suggest a device whose major impact has not yet occurred. If that is the case, then it is a cliché of limited value for local authorities discussing both the nature of their changing populations and the composition of their actual or potential workforce. The change is not going to occur – it has occurred already.

An examination of available census data for many local authorities makes it quite clear that the nature of the local population has changed very significantly in recent years. The data shown in Figure 2.4 indicate changing population patterns in Grampian region – from 1970 through to the early 1990s.

This is an area which has in some parts enjoyed thriving economic activity and pronounced growth, particularly in relation to the oil boom, but also through the development of other industries. This has been coupled with both household and family relocation, sustained growth of the number of young people requiring education, changing patterns of employment, and (in contrast to many other areas) a steady proportion of older people. Other local authorities have seen similar changes and have often found themselves hard pressed to keep up with those changes. Among Scottish housing authorities, for example, there are very few able to provide the amount of sheltered housing considered appropriate by Scottish Office advisers.

The other side of the demographic equation is the composition of the existing and potential workforce for local authorities. Employment trends in the 1970s and 1980s saw an increase in local authority employment driven predominantly by the recruitment of part-time female workers. As female labour participation rates in Britain have consistently run at a higher level than in many other European countries, and may now have peaked anyway, this source of potential employees is becoming less readily available. As other employers realise that such a process is occurring, they will be increasingly likely to provide conditions of employment that are – in individual and overall terms – more attractive to part-time women returners than those which local authorities currently provide. Similarly, a continuing decline in the number and proportion of younger people entering the labour market will make recruitment within that social group more difficult for local authorities.

As this passage is being written during a deep recession in which a typical advertisement for a local authority appointment may draw several hundred applications, this may seen a particularly foolish proposition. However, it is worth remembering that the principal reason why so many local authorities – particularly in the south of England – now operate some form of performance-related pay scheme is because they had considerable difficulty in recruiting staff in many different occupations and grades during the mid 1980s. Any significant upturn in the economy will again place these and other authorities in a similar position. The nature of our

FIGURE 2.4   **Changing age composition of Grampian Region**

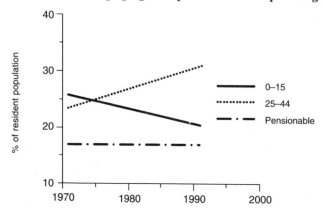

Sources: Office of Population Censuses and Surveys Census Report 1991; Census data – relevant years.

changing population and the likely projections of how that change
will continue is a matter of long-term consequence rather than short-
term inconvenience.

Social and behavioural change

Of equal long-term and lasting significance for many local authority
services and activities are the social and behavioural changes that
have occurred in the postwar period, and particularly from the mid
1960s onward, as our working and social lives came to assume a very
different character from those of our parents and neighbours who
came to adulthood before and during the Second World War. It is
foolish now – if it was every anything else – to write of the 'typical
family'. However, certain clear patterns of behaviour are observable
amongst individuals, domestic units and families of one kind or
another, and all of those changes have an impact on the local
authority and the way in which it organises itself to provide services.
This can be seen in any discussion of 'council housing'; in the past,
those who wished to be housed by the local authority were
frequently expected to demonstrate certain agreed standards of
behaviour; in many authorities for a long time it was only the
'better families' who were allocated local authority homes. Indeed,
the major programmes of house-building initiated during the 1920s
and 1930s specifically referred to 'artisans' housing'. During the
surge of major postwar rehousing, potential tenants were offered a
key to a house and expected simply to be grateful. There was no
expectation – either by the council or the tenant – that they might
wish to exercise some choice in relation to the house they lived in
and the area in which it was located.

   For a clear majority of those who are now seeking housing, either
on a first-time basis or through removal, housing with the local
authority is the last option they will seek. Rising expectations about
home ownership (even though dented by recent financial events) and
a personal taxation regime which, even in the middle of the house
price collapse, still makes financial sense for most people, means
that house purchase is the preferred option for the vast majority.
Table 2.2 shows changing social attitudes over recent years. That
change in attitude is compounded by government policies which
have consistently emphasised the private over the public and have

TABLE 2.2 Expectations of home ownership (%)

Year	1985	1986	1989	1990	1991
Buy next home	59	68	68	71	63
Rent from local authority	23	18	13	10	16
Rent from other landlord	11	9	11	14	15

Source: R. Jowell *et al.*, *British Social Attitudes – The 9th Report*, (London: Dartmouth, 1992).

had their greatest impact in public spending terms in recent years on housing provision. Housing is the most striking example of the way in which our perception of local authority services has generally changed. There are however many other services in which there is an increasing expectation of individual choice, of the possibility that the consumer of the local authority service should be offered something better than the basic, rather utilitarian, provision that has often characterised local authority services in the past. So, in libraries, swimming pools, sports facilities, a far wider variety of provision is made.

Individuals and communities no longer see that what the local authority does must be accepted, or at best resentfully tolerated. There is now a far greater willingness to challenge local authority actions, to argue an alternative course of action, and in many cases to do so with the support of members and officials within the council or within other organisations with which the council has to work.

The changing family

Although it is possible to demonstrate that there is no such thing as the 'typical family' it is nonetheless clear that the concept of that idealised family still exists and has a significant influence on policy aspiration and formulation. It is still not unusual to hear in a discussion within local authorities that 'we should be building more family homes' whenever housing programmes are discussed. When major planning proposals and developments are being debated, particularly where based on retail businesses, there will be at least one member of the planning committee who will intervene with a

comment about 'of course these aren't real jobs'. In both such
instances, it seems clear that the assumption being made is that the
typical family unit combines a man (who provides the major source
of income), a woman (who, if she has a job, does not have a 'real
job') and two or more children. This mythical typical family has of
course been just that – mythical – for many years now. Figure 2.5
illustrates the trend over recent years.

FIGURE 2.5   Changing household composition in Great Britain

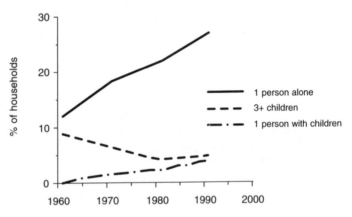

Sources: Office of Population Censuses and Surveys Census Report 1991;
Census data – relevant years.

The implications of this for many different elements of local
authority policy and provision are only now becoming more clearly
understood. In housing, there continues to be in most local
authorities a gross underprovision of smaller – and indeed very
large – units, with the bulk of accommodation being made up of
housing designed for just that 'typical family'. The operational
practices that underpin the way in which the school system is run
usually seem to assume that if children are sent home early, or
school timetables are changed at short notice, there will be somebody at home to handle that. Care for older people was often
planned on the assumption that there would be nearby family and
relatives who could (and would) provide informal care for the
person concerned at home or in a home-related setting.

A movable feast?

It has been observed that for many years one of the underlying assumptions that characterised thought and discussion about any possible reorganisation of local government was the requirement that the separation between town and country be retained. None-theless, the activities of the pre-1970 English Boundary Commission, and the two reorganisations of the mid 1970s in England and Wales and in Scotland, were forced in various ways to acknowledge the extending influence of urban settlements and the increased mobility of those who lived outside the concentrated urban areas. An often expressed resentment of those who lived in the large towns and cities was that their country neighbours would come in and attend the theatre, visit the library, and swim in the swimming pool without being willing to pay the cost of supporting these activities. If anything, this increased mobility has become more pronounced since the reorganisations of the mid 1970s. People travel further to work, they travel in different ways, and a large proportion of them still expect to travel by car rather than by forms of mass public transport.

It is not only everyday travel that is having a significant impact on the way in which local authorities are organised; so are the longer-term consequences of increased geographical mobility. Even where there are extended families, those families are increasingly separated by long distances or difficult travel. For younger and older members of the family, reliance on the active adult members is no longer something that can be taken for granted. This has its impact on care for the elderly, both for the 'younger' elderly and for those who are considered to be very old and frail. It also has implications for services such as schooling, where increasing numbers of children have parents who are separated and perhaps with another partner. In practical terms, when parental preference for schooling is determined by address and proximity to the favoured school, it is difficult to know which parental address the child lives at. As consumers of all services, including schooling, become more asser-tive in their right to choice and in their determination of what is appropriate for their children, this is increasingly becoming to be an issue which is troubling for both educational managers and legal advisers.

The changing user of public services

The changing expectations of service users

When we discuss local government services today, it is apparent that we actually have great difficulty in finding appropriate words to describe and define those people who use and benefit from those services. Walsh (1988, p. 10) has claimed: 'the words we have are simply inadequate'. So we describe users of local authorities as users, clients, consumers, citizens; even punters, Joe public, and – still – ratepayers. Increasingly, the word used is customer. The growing popularity of that last word in many local government circles has not gone unchallenged, and it is still a term which many people are not comfortable with. Nonetheless, the fact that we are using such a variety of different words to describe those people who benefit from local authority services is itself symptomatic of the extent to which the public are now defined differently by the council, and the 'public' now perceive local authority services in a different manner from the way in which they did twenty, thirty or forty years ago. It is no longer assumed that the local authority is the sole provider of services; it is no longer taken for granted that the local authority will automatically be 'right' or at least able to achieve what it wishes at the expense of the individual or his or her household.

In short, the public are no longer deferential and accepting consumers of whatever service the local authority chooses to provide. Those who have a choice – and their number is growing – will increasingly opt for the opportunity to make that choice. In some service areas, such as the provision of education for children with special needs, pre-school education, and care for older relatives, individuals are now often assertive – sometimes to the point of aggression – in demanding what they perceive as being appropriate levels of service and care for their relatives. Many users of public services view themselves as 'consumers', with the opportunities and rights associated with that status.

Universality or segmentation?

There are many different historical streams that led to the establishment of elected local government in the various parts of Britain. In any reference to the historical origins of local government the emphasis is on a variety of activities that are, generally speaking, universal in their nature (Stoker, 1991, pp. 1–3) - for example, the variety of single-purpose bodies responsible for major roads and 'improvements', and rudimentary forms of public order. The early years of local government were characterised by a predominance of spending on those infrastructural and public order services which made the greatest significant difference to the standard of life – and indeed even the lifespan – of many citizens. Those facilities were concerned with addressing what the economists call 'externalities' - that is, those elements of our environment which require a collective and universal solution. Figure 2.6 illustrates this trend.

As the pattern of provision of local government services has changed, increasingly rapidly, towards a more individualised form of provision, so the management challenge for local government has become ever more difficult. Large public, publicly accountable and therefore bureaucratic organisations are – though some would dispute this – generally agreed to be the most appropriate organisa-

FIGURE 2.6   Spending on major public services, 1885–1975

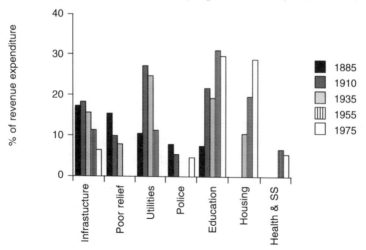

Source: figures in G. Stoker, 'Creating a Local Government for a Post-Fordist Society', in G. Stoker and J. Stewart (eds), *The Future of Local Government* (London: Macmillan, 1989).

tions to provide just that range of universal infrastructural and support services needed by a complex modern society. It is however apparent that there is a growing measure of doubt about their capacity to provide the individualised and customised services which an increasingly diverse pattern of social and individual demands may deem is appropriate for social life in the late twentieth century. Thus, for example, whilst there may be debate about the best way to organise a particular service, it seems reasonably clear that an agency such as the local authority is the most appropriate organisational form for the collection of rubbish, cleaning of streets, and repair and maintainance of highways. It is not clear that most local authorities are particularly well organised to provide, for example, a video film hire facility. Most of those who want and use that type of service make a spontaneous choice in the early evening; the best way for them to make that choice is to drop in to a convenient location, browse, see what is available and then take it away on a short-term basis with the minimum of necessary complication in doing so. Where library services provided by the local authority have attempted to compete in this area they have not been conspicuously successful – and have sometimes found this to be at the cost of other functions and activities. It may prove difficult for local authorities to think increasingly in terms of patterns of individual choice and how to respond to that, but it is a process to which they will increasingly have to adjust.

Summary

The past thirty or forty years have seen dramatic changes in local government; changes which accelerated and took on a more aggressive form through the recent years of Conservative government. These changes are often irreversible, because we live in a different society from that of the 1940s and 1950s. Even if reversible, it is unlikely that either this government or a future alternative government will reverse them. For these reasons, the challenge of effectively managing a changing council is going to become ever more central for those who are concerned to make their careers in local government. The following chapters explore in some detail how these people can meet the challenge.

Some points for discussion

1. In what ways have you noticed local government services changing in recent years?
2. Has local government in your area ever been 'non-political'?
3. Have you noticed changes in expenditure in local government? What form have they taken?
4. Are there 'gaps' in local government services in your community? What are they?

3 Managing Services

Who are the managers in local government?

As one study has observed, management in Britain has often been viewed as a lower order activity:

> To the British, management has always been more of a practical art rather than an applied science. It is a word moreover with a rather lowly pedigree; to 'manage' in colloquial English usage means usually to 'cope' whilst 'manager' was traditionally a title reserved for the more mundane service functions ('transport manager', 'catering manager') rather then for the senior roles in an organisation (Handy *et al.*, 1988, p. 7).

As in industry and commerce, no less so in local government. For many years, and particularly in the period prior to the reorganisations of the 1972 and 1973 local government acts, the ambitious person appointed to a local authority with aspirations to reach the top knew clearly which post he or she was aiming for. The architect wanted to be county architect; the librarian to be city librarian; the educational official to be chief education officer. Indeed the epitome of success in local government, the top post within the authority, was usually titled – paradoxically – town or county *clerk*. Such a focus on the professional roots and background of the most senior posts was highly significant, both for the management of the organisation and the careers of the managers within it. At the strategic level of the authority, the definition of the management task, even in the reorganised local authorities post-1974 and 1975, was seen as being constrained by the powers and assumptions of that professional tradition.

The strategic managers

The Bains Report of 1972 recommended to the newly established local authorities the manner in which they might organise themselves to accommodate the demands of a changing world and changed organisational form. The recommendations of the report appear to have been widely accepted amongst local councils, as were those of the comparable and parallel report for Scottish local government (Paterson, 1973). Interestingly, however, few authorities appear to have heeded the sound advice contained in the foreword of the report: 'If every . . . newly appointed officer . . . studies this report carefully and sees that those suggestions appropriate are applied to the work of his new authority then local government in the future is going to be far more efficient and effective than ever before' (Bains, 1972, p. vii). Many councils adopted the Bains and Paterson proposals as formulae or patterns rather than considering whether the suggestions were 'appropriate'. In determining the job description for their new chief executives the majority of councils did so either by adopting the model job description contained in each report or by modifying these in some way.

The role that the Bains Committee saw for the chief executive reflected the broad trend of thinking about a more effective approach to the rational planning of local public services. This had been developed through, for example, the 1960s report of the Committee on the Management of Local Government (Maud, 1967) and the discussion initiated by various academic institutions, individual academics and professional organisations. Among the many recommendations of the Bains report, some of the most significant relate to the appointment of the most senior staff of a council. The chief executive was to be 'leader of the officers of the authority and *principal adviser* to the Council on matters of general policy' (Bains, 1972, p. 125, emphasis added). It seems that, despite the apparent widespread and sometimes uncritical acceptance of the recommendations of the Bains report, in many authorities such ideas were simply a cladding on the more traditional relationships at the top of the organisation. Alexander (1982b) describes this phenomenon in his study of post-reorganisation local government and suggests that in various councils the role of the chief executive can be described as being fulfilled by the occupant in either a 'weak' or 'strong' manner. In effect, the 'strong' chief executives defined their task as a *managerial* one, shaping and disposing the resources of the authority in support of the collective purpose; the 'weak' chief executive adopted a coordinating role, allowing chief officers to drive the policy development and implementation process from their departmental perspective.

Practice and convention change over time, as different occupants fill posts within a council and attempt to establish their own approach to the duties associated with those posts. The former county and town clerks in some councils had developed their role in a manner which may have led them to see clear evolutionary links between the 'town clerk' of 1973 and the 'chief executive' of 1975. Some of the new chief executives developed their role in a pro-active manner which clearly established their position as the senior member of an authority's paid staff, in practice as in title. Others appear to have confined their interpretation of the professional and statutory discretion of chief officers very loosely. In doing so they may have allowed departmental initiative to flourish, but often at the expense of corporate purpose.

Over the period of the 1980s and the early 1990s however, as increasing resource and organisational pressures were placed upon councils, a shift in perception and attitude developed. The post of chief executive was increasingly defined with an *expectation* that the occupant demonstrated a pro-active and leading role. The government response to the deliberations of the Widdicombe Committee, in prescribing that councils should establish a post of 'head of paid service' rather than a chief executive perhaps represents the only exception to that generally observable trend (Widdicombe, 1986a). In increasing numbers of councils there is an explicit assumption that a new chief executive will assume a more overtly managerial role in relation to the general operation of the council. Often the formal described duties, as expressed in the job description and associated papers, are only marginally and subtly different from the standard 'Bains' or 'Bains rephrased' job descriptions of the mid 1970s. However, they *are* different, and the expectation is much greater.

There are of course many other factors which have an impact on this changing role for the chief executive, including the increasing incidence of purposeful member involvement in the strategic direction of the authority. The best of chief executives perform effectively precisely because they *can* manage in that milieu. There are recent examples of how the process of change is affecting the manner in which the post of chief executive is defined and assessed. The 'job purpose' of the chief executive of Bedfordshire County uses the word 'manager' or 'management' in three of the five key functions. It specifically states that the chief executive is: 'the Council's most senior manager with management responsibility over all other Chief Officers' (Bedfordshire County Council, 1991). In Tayside Region, changes in the management and operation of the council were foreshadowed by the commissioning of a consultancy report which indicated that the most effective course of action for the council would be the strengthening of the role of the chief executive, allied to an increased expectation of enhanced accountability for all senior managers (Tayside Regionional Council, 1990).

Such changes can be difficult for the people undergoing – and initiating – the process of transition. Rosemary Stewart (1991) describes three stages in a managerial career, the most senior of which, 'the general manager' is perhaps analogous to the post of chief executive. Indeed, the terms in which she describes this type of appointment will be readily recognisable to any chief executive or those who work with a chief executive: 'responsibility for several functions which are likely to include one or more that are unfamiliar. When that happens the general manager has to learn how to manage without such knowledge; he must not be scared of others' expertise, nor allow them to put him off by talking in specialist language' (p. 10). This quotation echoes the observation made in an interview by the chief executive of a district council. 'I knew I had to struggle hard to get to grips with finance; I don't understand the technicalities – but that's his job – but after a year I have a good idea of the broad principle we are working to' (private interview).

The Stewart quotation helps to set in context some of the other dynamic forces that are affecting local government at present. The emphasis of the most senior posts shifts towards a perception of the role as being concerned with setting the strategic direction of the authority and creating an appropriate management climate and organisational culture. At other levels within the organisation there are increased expectations of managers being required to assume more responsibilities for the disposition of resources and the achievement of the objectives defined for them. Tayside Region now emphasises and encourages the 'accountability' of the hundred or so top managers within the organisation (Tayside Regional Council, 1990). Kent County Council, a controversial model for some local authorities but one which has often set a path which others have followed, has placed considerable weight on the devolution of management functions between and within departments. 'Not only are central departments pushing responsibility for the management of the key resources out to service delivery departments, responsibility is also being pushed down the line to as close to the point of service delivery as possible. . ... In the process, management structures have been flattened with levels of unnecessary management stripped out' (Frater, 1992, p. 10). Such changes place the greatest day-to-day pressure upon and emphasise the significance of another group of key managers within local government: the operational managers.

The operational managers

The corollary of defining the most senior posts in local government in terms of a professional background was that for many years posts to which the name 'manager' were attached were relatively low-status posts. They were often in low-grade functional areas divorced from the mainstream professions of local government. Such people were baths managers, works managers, transport managers and catering managers. Such a distinction, and the social attitudes associated with it, was captured very well in a detailed study of the work of the chief education officer (Kogan, 1974) which quoted one CEO as saying: 'and so an Education officer finds himself looking after the education of children and the welfare of the community but to some extent he's also a transport manager, and a catering manager, and he has all manner of other such sidelines that he must attend to' (Kogan, 1974, p. 49).

The core status of a senior white collar post was expressed in relation to the base professional function and to a relatively well-defined benchmark grade of organisational status. So somebody responsible for a several groups of architectural staff, and still working at the drawing-board, would be described as senior principal architect. Similarly a senior member of staff within an education department responsible for special education may be senior assistant director of education (job advertisements, *Guardian*, February/March 1992). Where new developments within the authority or within local government generally have forced the organisation to reshape and reform itself, staff are often keen to cling on to the certainties bestowed by convention. One study of economic development activities in Scottish local authorities (Kerley, 1989) indicated how this strategic function was being developed by local government, frequently outside the framework of the conventional department headed by a director. Yet interviews carried out as part of this study yielded several examples of senior staff in economic development units who would spontaneously claim that, for example 'This post [economic development manager] is of assistant director status, you know.'

Despite the attachments of comfort and status associated with the professionally derived title it is clear that in increasing numbers of senior council staff are being designated 'managers'. It seems likely that this is a reflection at operational level of the broader changes that are occurring in local government. In more and more councils, responsibility and authority are being extended downwards into the organisation, and staff with the responsibility for particular functions are expected to manage that function. This is of course an uneven process, and the pace and extent of change varies even within those councils at the leading edge of this process. A politically controversial decision may be made, a error of judgement occurs, temporary financial constraints override the general drive to delegate decisions and responsibility. Nonetheless, in councils across Britain the general trend of development appears clear – more and more people are being appointed as 'managers', because that is what they are now expected to do. For some that may involve a dramatic and sometimes difficult change in expectation and working practice.

A Local Government Training Board publication summarised the experience of Cambridgeshire County Council in changing its management culture and processes (Local Government Training Board, 1988). That council was encouraging managers to engage in risk-taking to achieve results; to focus on the task rather than the procedures of administration; and to be flexible in their approach. Such an idea requires senior staff to create a climate of trust and flexibility for those managers to work within.

It is clear that an increasing number of councils now describe staff as 'managers'. By implication, they will expected to fulfil a different range of duties within that post from those which would have attached to it in the past, *or* to carry out those duties in a different way. A study of a major recruitment medium for senior local government staff yielded a significant number of advertisements for posts that used the title 'manager' in a way that they probably would not have done four or five years previously. In one edition (*Guardian*, 12 February 1992) a social services department was advertising for a domiciliary care manager to 'lead the management of a team providing . . . services'. A district finance department sought a revenues manager (rents). They were looking for an 'experienced manager for this post, as did a London borough in their advertisement for a divisional business manager for the social services department. In some respects it may be that the adoption of such job titles represent a fashion which may have no lasting impact. Indeed, a close study of the job descriptions associated with these and other such posts suggest that this may be the case. In some cases posts appear to have simply been retitled, without reconsideration of the range of duties associated with the job; responsibilities are on occasion unclear, with considerable use of words such as 'liaise' and 'review' rather than the unequivocal expression of accountability and responsibility one might assume would be attached to closely defined management roles. The inclusion of phrases such as 'to manage all resources within a particular service provision area . . . and . . . take responsibility for the performance of that service plan' is found in only a minority of instances.

It is not appropriate here to engage in a minute textual analysis of job advertisements and job descriptions, but both are important elements in establishing the management climate within an authority, as are the other public signals that an organisation gives about itself and what it expects of its staff. They give a clear message about the council as employer and organisation, and they give the first indication to a potential candidate what the organisation expects of the person appointed. What they do not tell either the candidate or the external commentator is what managers actually do in their jobs; this is the subject of the next section of the chapter.

What do managers do when they manage?

Much has been written about what managers do when they manage; major studies have been based on diary exercises, observation and interviews. Much has been written by successful managers either post-career or mid-career, and although most of this genre is based on experience in the industrial sector it has some considerable value for those who are interested in the broader climate of managerial change. Standard management textbooks survey and summarize much of this material, often setting it in the context of a very traditional model of the management process. Such a model is often derived from the classical works of management, and has been highly influential in shaping how local government thinks about management. Many of the assumptions that underlie the way in which local authorities have traditionally thought about their overall organisation, the structuring of management hierarchies and pay systems for staff owe much to this classical tradition. A significant factor in this is the importation of such traditions through the practice of management consultancies, and the adoption of proprietary job evaluation schemes.

For many managers in local government, the contrast between what they actually do, what they see their colleagues and superiors doing, and what they *think* managers should be doing can cause frustration, anger and pronounced distress. At a minimum, all readers will have had the experience of hearing somebody say (or themselves saying) – 'If it wasn't for all of these meetings I could get on with my *real* work'. At worst they will have observed the competent – even outstanding – architect, social worker, accountant, not performing effectively as a manager and written off five years later as 'dead wood'. Why? What is it that managers do, and what should they do, that the task can seem so difficult?

For many managers in local government, the competing demands of the job are made far more difficult to reconcile by the strains imposed by the accelerating pace of external change, which forces organisations to reshape themselves almost constantly.We can however begin to define both what it is that operational managers in councils are expected to do, and the roles they fulfil which enable them to do those tasks. We can attempt this by looking at the various job descriptions for council 'manager' posts advertised in *The Guardian* during February 1992, and comparing them with data obtained from a survey of local authority staff attending a series of management courses (Kerley, 1993d).

Mintzberg in his famous and still persuasive study of the manager's job, proposed that there were ten elements within the role of manager, though the balance would vary with different jobs (and over time within the same job, given the discretionary elements that characterise managerial time-use). These were:

Figurehead
Leader
Liaison
Information monitor
Information disseminator
Spokesman
Entrepreneur
Disturbance handler
Resource allocator
Negotiator

His work was based on the experience of senior managers, in both public and private sectors, in North America. Whilst all of the above roles are clearly relevant to the most senior staff in an authority – chief executives and directors – the blend of roles may be significantly different for operational managers within the council. For the most senior staff, the array of roles described will tend to be skewed toward those which help set the climate for the organisation – the figurehead and leadership roles. People in such positions describe their roles in this way: 'I was appointed to give a message to the entire organisation – to make changes' (district chief executive); 'I think it's very important that I get around departments, to show face and let them know what I – and the council – want done' (region chief executive). Below I examine the way in which some operational managers see their own roles within the organisation, within the aim of understanding the managerial tasks that councils expect managers to do – as outlined in their job descriptions. Such job descriptions are a blend of elements: some comprise detailed prescriptions for the performance of the job – with 28 separate clauses in one for a community alarm service manager – and others emphasising more general performance outcomes. However, close analysis of several of these documents supports the greater part of the Mintzberg thesis on managerial roles.

As a *figurehead*, an area family services manager is expected to 'represent the department at community and public meetings'.

The expectation that a security and environmental manager will: 'demonstrate leadership and motivational skills, developing participation and teamwork . . . and remain visible and accessible to all personnel' is clearly establishing that the postholder will act as a *leader*.

A community alarm service manager is expected to '*liaise* with resident wardens bodies and charities . . . lettings . . . and other departments.

A divisional business manager in social services has responsibilities that require the postholder to 'co-ordinate management *information and monitor* results'.

It is still clear that in many councils the public face of the authority is limited to a very small number of people, whether members or senior staff, and therefore the expectation that managers will act as the *spokesman* for the council is rarely stated.

The concept of the local authority manager as *entrepreneur* is in many respects alien to the traditions of public administration, consistency and accountability which have characterised public services in the past. Whilst it is a novelty in most local authorities it is not unknown, and Paul Sabin of Kent has argued publicly that 'I wanted a more entrepreneurial approach to the job [of council managers]' (Hegarty, 1992). One of the job descriptions studied (security and environmental manager) includes the following among the principal duties. 'To be innovative and entrepreneurial in terms of service delivery and anticipation of future customer needs, with more freedom and responsibility devolved to team leaders and professional support staff to deal with operational issues.'

The role of *disturbance handler* is perhaps characterised by the usual expectation that the manager will be the first line of contact for complaints from service users, and from staff. 'To undertake disciplinary and grievance interviews for officer staff', is one feature of the job description for a resource centre manager.

To be a *resource allocator* implies a degree of *control* over the disposition of resources which is usually highly circumscribed in the context of local government. Individuals may typically claim to be responsible for either major capital projects or substantial revenue expenditure, but such 'responsibility' is frequently hedged around with a wide variety of restrictions and constraints, as the following example from a job description for the post of security and environmental manager makes clear. 'To manage all resources within a particular service area, or possibly a number of areas, in an efficient, effective and economic manner and within a framework of corporate and departmental policies and priorities. These resources will include personnel, premises, equipment, furniture, vehicles and finance, etc., and demand particular expertise in timecosting, recharges to costs centres and budgetary control.'

The image of the *negotiator* as a heavy-fisted male pounding the table and demanding enhanced overtime rates is a hard one to escape. Yet for most managers either inter- or intra-agency negotiation (particularly in services subject to scarcity, rationing and allocation criteria) is the stuff of day-to-day routine, even if not expressed as such, as in this description of the duties of a group manager – for day nurseries. 'To confirm, negotiate, liaise with other Services and Departments, especially Education and Health, in order to ensure that appropriate alternatives and additional services have been considered in order to best meet the needs of children placed.'

In effect, those whom we have called 'operational managers' are often described as 'middle managers', a phrase which is not particularly helpful in local government, with its complexity of grading structures and wide patterns of job responsibility. What such people do have in common with the middle manager in the trading sector is that their job is changing rapidly, as increased demands are placed upon them by the organisation. The nature of such changes throughout the economy is unclear and, appears to vary both within sectors and within organisations. Two observers of the process have suggested that the following characteristics of the changes are significant for local government (Dopson and Stewart, 1989b). There appears in many settings to be a reduction in the number of layers of management, coupled with an actual reduction in the number of people in such positions. This is accompanied by increased responsibilities – formally – for those in such positions; and enhanced information systems mean that results are more visible. There was a wide range of responsibilities attached to such posts and an increased span of control expected of postholders.

From the research reported, these patterns of change are apparently more difficult for managers in the public services to accept than they are for their counterparts in the private sector. Several reasons are suggested for this, among them the perception of a clear need for change, which is plainly regarded as a competitive threat rather than simply a political decision. If change is seen as a frequent and usual phenomenon it is more readily accepted. It is also helpful if the organisation puts considerable effort into explaining and communicating change – often a neglected area in some local authorities. Of the greatest significance for this book is the authors' assessment that one of the major barriers to effective acceptance of change is: 'whether the managers see themselves primarily as professionals, as many do in the public sector, or primarily as managers' (Dopson and Stewart, 1989a, p. 26). This observation of the importance of the professional orientation as a factor in hindering adaptability to change is not confined to this country, as commentators in other countries confirm. But it has major implications for the way in which local government recruits, develops and socialises its managers in their positions, and what messages it then gives about what it expects of managers.

The transition to management

It is a frequent observation that professionalism and departmentalism are a great strength of local government – and also a great weakness. A defining characteristic of the way in which local government has been shaped is that it remained unchallenged for many years, and in the majority of councils remains unchallenged. An observation from John Stewart more than twenty years ago confirms the enduring strength of this phenomenon. 'Professionalism has contributed much to local government and will contribute more if it is recognised that there are other and wider bases for a personnel policy. The professional can no more rely on professionalism alone that can the non-professional' (Stewart, 1971, p. 88).

One of the significant factors discussed by Stewart is the extent to which local government recruits initially from a professional base and with the clear intention of developing personnel through a professional framework. One of the attractions and strengths of local government and the other public services for many ambitious young graduates is the support provided through post-initial training. Local government and the public services are the largest area of professional recruitment in this country – indeed, for many professions they are either the preferred option for post-qualifying appointment (social work and teaching) or a source of sound and varied work experience at some point in any professional career (most of the land-based professions). This firm professional base to recruitment into local government contrasts sharply with managerial recruitment and development in the trading sector where graduate recruitment is typically aimed at recruiting potential managers from a broad range of educational backgrounds.

It also reflects upon the manner in which local authorities organise the support and development of their staff once within the organisation. Most local authorities have well-established and well-supported patterns of post-qualifying training for staff in their professional field, with the chartered professions being particularly well sustained. A study by the Local Government Management Board (1990) suggested that almost all local authorities (97 per cent) gave partly qualified professionals the chance to complete their training. This does not always rest easily with a broader authority-wide focus on developing managerial skills and attitudes: 'There are therefore two quite separate initiatives happening simultaneously within authorities: management development and professional development. Authorities attempting to develop management skills often find tension between the two. . . . The result is that the development of professional skills is taking place outside the authority's strategic policy' (Local Government Management Board, 1990, pp. 28–9).

These perceived tensions are a reflection both of an older tradition of professionalism and of the underlying tension that still exists in many councils between the centre (the focus of strategic thinking about management in the council) and the departments (the focus of both service delivery and the professional ethos). It is also apparent, from contact with many local authorities, that it is not coincidence that funds for management development in the council are often held in the centre, while funds for professional training are controlled by the departments.

What are the implications of these different factors in thinking about the position and development of the manager in local government? It does suggest that the pattern of experience in many authorities, and in local government as a whole, is close to the 'Darwinian system of development' that Handy *et al.* (1988, p. 7) observed in British management: those who adapt, survive. The forces at play here are complex, but it is possible to obtain a better understanding of how people manage now in local government, and how they might be helped to manage more effectively, if we consider how their management careers have probably developed.

As suggested above, the most frequent path of recruitment into the management streams of local government is through a 'professional' background, usually involving graduate or quasi-graduate entry-status. Even where the entrant is a school-leaver, then the encouragement to obtain professional training and qualification transforms that person into somebody who is recognisably a professional by the time he or she is, say, twenty-two or twenty-three. Examples from both the middle of the organisation and the top illustrate that process. Alexander (1982b, p. 73) describes the background of chief executives in the late 1970s and shows fewer than one per cent from a background ('Others') that is not clearly professional in nature and equivalent to graduate status. Of the group of operational managers studied as part of the background research for this book, 84 per cent have a degree, postgraduate or professional qualification.

Such a person enters the local authority as a professional and works as an architect, engineer, accountant or planner for some two or three years, depending on the nature and requirements of post-qualifying experience. They do well, perform competently, and demonstrate a pattern of hard work, enthusiasm, and initiative – or perhaps they just 'keep their nose clean'. This person is then, after perhaps as little as two years at the job, promoted into a more senior position with responsibility for a range of resources, including, critically, other professionals. They enter the 'hyphenated career structure' and become a 'professional–manager' (Gunn, 1992).

The vital factor in this process is that a combination of those 'Darwinian processes' described by Handy and the emphasis of the professional background and training mean that, more often than not, little provision is made to equip such people for the critical transfer into the first management post. It is not an exaggeration to claim that for many current managers in local government their first promotion saw them leave the office on Friday as a 'professional' and return Monday as a 'professional-manager'. They had neither training, support, nor counselling – simply an assumption that they would 'get on with it' whatever 'it' might be. In Handy's terms: 'the effective manager would emerge and the ineffective would be weeded out. Character, initiative, energy and imagination have always been more important words in the British managerial tradition than knowledge or intellect' (Handy *et al.*, 1988, p. 7).

Unfortunately for these new managers – and for the council that employs them – the nature of the managerial task is not as obvious as might be thought. It is certainly not most readily understood by observing what your predecessor did, or what your colleagues do. A simple experiment will confirm this for any manager: observe the work pattern of somebody a year into a management job and it will be apparent that – in the majority of instances – he or she is actually doing a range of things significantly different to what the previous incumbent did. One of the prime – and prized – characteristics of the management role is discretion in the use of time and energy; a discretion that increases as the career advances. Apart from any other factors, in such a period of rapid change and organisational restructuring, there may not be any previous incumbent of the post! The uncertainty as to what is involved in the managerial task, and the increased degree of discretion over use of time and energy, can lead to considerable uncertainty. Torrington and Weightman (1989, p. 120) describe the impact of this transition:

> Early in their careers middle managers acquire a body of knowl-edge and technical skill to qualify and practice as pharmacist, engineer, teacher, or whatever specialist career was followed. The jobs could not be done without that knowledge, and more specific information could always be obtained to solve an unexpected problem so that an answer could always be found.
>
> When they cross over to the better paid, higher ranking (and logically more skillful) activity of managing, they expect the new activity to have a similar body of expertise: reliable, explicit and accessible.

The process of distancing involved in this was graphically – and ruefully – described by one such person, a senior architect who claimed: 'Yes, I recognise that. . . . I still have a drawing board in the office, but the last time I used it was to plan the family holidays' (private interview). The final career break for the vast majority of people in such career patterns is the promotion to 'manager'. Such a person is an accountant who no longer runs a ledger; a social worker who does not see clients; the teacher who no longer teaches, and an architect who no longer designs on a drawing board. In effect, they have followed the career path which is demonstrated simply in Figure 3.1.

There are clear consequences which flow from this model of the classical local government management career. The most apparent is that people in this developmental channel – pace the architect cited above – are forced to surrender areas of work they were trained in and good at in exchange for areas of work they are probably not trained in and may not be very good at. The balance of their workload will change, and this proposition is supported by the group of operational managers who were asked about their work as

FIGURE 3.1 Management career development

Professional

▼

Professional– Manager

▼

Manager– Professional

▼

Manager

part of the background for this book. These people were specifically asked about the balance of their routine workload between the 'professional' and the 'managerial', and whether they could suggest in proportional terms what that balance was. All those who responded to a postal questionnaire (126 in total) were able to answer and the average proportion of time spent on managerial tasks was 59 per cent with the remaining 41 per cent of time spent on professional tasks. The range was of course far wider, with one person stating that no working time was spent on professional tasks (an assistant director of education who had previously been a teacher) and another with only 10 per cent of time spent on managerial tasks (a planner).The implications of a progressive change of work pattern such as that shown in Figure 3.2 are highly significant for the way in which the management of local government is changing, sometimes with conflicting and contradictory consequences for the professionals involved;

- They may become remote from the practice of the work they are responsible for, and therefore forced to ensure subordinate compliance with their requests/ instructions through the authority of their position rather than any sense of confidence in their experience and competence.

FIGURE 3.2   The changing balance of professional and managerial demands

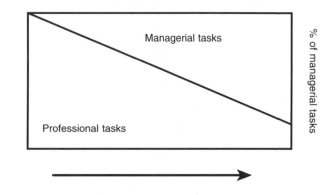

Time/management career development

- Alternatively, faced with uncertainty they may find solace in retreating to the 'comfort zone' of professional tasks they are confident of, and ignore the managerial tasks they are now *meant* to do.
- They need to justify their position to both superiors and subordinates in terms of their contribution to the organisational purpose and therefore support – and even create – procedures and systems which are literally self-serving in that they duplicate existing information systems.

People in such a position are often trapped between demands and pressures from above and those from below. They have suffered in the past from an organisation and superiors within the organisation which have literally suppressed their potential talents and their contribution to organisational goals. That has happened because *their* superiors have been locked into implementing controls and procedures according to the traditional view of a public organisation in which process and procedure are often more important that outcome. Previous assumptions and processes have encouraged managers – and staff at all levels – to downgrade their expectations and to operate at the lower levels of potential performance.

Figure 3.3 suggests that most jobs can be seen as comprising three elements. The routinely accomplished elements of the post comprise the greater part of the workload – the middle section of the diagram. These are the tasks broadly appropriate to the post and the person within it. The lower portion of the diagram, which may perhaps comprise up to 20 per cent of the routine conditioned workload are tasks which are so easily done by the incumbent that they could – and should – be done by somebody else! The top section of the column are those parts of the work which an employee is conscious of finding demanding, stretching, and ultimately developmental in their impact. They are the tasks and projects which are taken on with a degree of hesitancy and trepidation, because that they could be difficult and challenging. Good managers, good organisations, and people conscious of their career development are always striving to push up the range of tasks and take on projects and activities which are a challenge. Poor managers and poor organisations are always pressing people down the range.

It is important for local authorities to release that talent, as a matter of routine expectation for all those who fill management positions within the council. It requires the organisation, and the people who lead it, to develop that kind of public service culture which is characterised by Stewart and Clarke (1987) as the 'public service orientation'. Some studies have suggested that the shift to a culture of high performance in public agencies is achieved through a number of channels: close interdependence between different parts of the organisation, good contact with top management; perceptions of fair remuneration; and good opportunities for employee development. Observation would suggest that the most effective of our local authorities are moving in those directions. The most effective of the strategic managers are encouraging their operational managers to stretch their way up the scale of tasks outlined in Figure 3.3, seeking to make them accountable and responsible. The best of the operational managers are pushing their way up that scale, relishing and enjoying that accountability. We earlier quoted the view of a chief education officer to support the argument that the professional background of many senior staff in local government had in the past

FIGURE 3.3   Balancing the individual work load

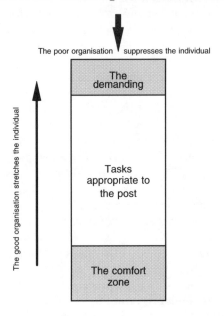

devalued and downgraded the management process within the organisation. To close this chapter, it is perhaps appropriate to cite another CEO from the same study who suggests, 'There are two kinds of management, I would say. One is the controlling or regulating, seeing that it doesn't become rusty in your terms, and the other is dynamic. And I would prefer to regard my job as being not a controller but infusing or directing the machine to new enterprises' (Kogan, 1974, p. 149).

Summary

This chapter has sought to outline the increased focus on the management process and the role of the manager in local government since the late 1970s. This has had an impact on managers at the top strategic level of the council, and on operational managers. For both groups it has meant an increased emphasis on an active purposeful pursuit of council, departmental and unit objectives and performance. It has required a shift from the predominantly professional focus which previously characterised local government and has caused problems of transition for many. This transition is helped if those involved are able to understand the process of career development council managers need to go through, and appreciate the implications for them, for the organisation and for their staff.

Some points for discussion

1. Who are the managers in local government?
2. Does a professional background help a manager – or hinder?
3. Does it help your understanding of management to think of a manager filling different roles as part of the managerial job?
4. What specific knowledge, skills and abilities would you look for in a manager for a service you are familiar with?
5. Can we reconcile managerial discretion and freedom with public accountability?

4 Managing People

It is common to find all large organisations, in both the public and private sectors, suggesting their most important asset to be the people who work for the organization. Typical is the claim made by a metropolitan district: 'Employees are the councils most vital resource in delivering quality. *'Our Vision for Kirklees'* explains that they must have recognition and reward for good performance and real opportunities to develop. Another priority for the year ahead is to ensure that employees at all levels have the opportunity to contribute their experience to the improvement of the services' (Kirklees Metropolitan Council, 1991, p. 1) Similarly, amongst Scottish Regional Councils, a recent annual report from Lothian Region claims that: 'the council recognises that the delivery of high quality, cost effective services depends on its workforce – its biggest asset – and is committed to using its staffing resources as effectively and efficiently as possible' (Lothian Regional Council, 1992, p. 12).

Indeed, the increased emphasis on people as an asset to organisations has directly underpinned the creation of a government-led drive to improve the quality of support for staff and staffing among many different types of employee organisation. In 1991 the Department of Employment established 'Investors in People'. As the background papers for this initiative claim: 'the crucial importance of people to business success is now almost universally recognised by companies, but there is a huge gap between recognising this and knowing exactly what to do about it. Hence, Investors in People, which aims to help companies bridge this gap' (Foster, 1992).

The importance that is attached to effective management of people is also recognised elsewhere. The Management Charter Initiative puts first in its code of practice 'to improve leadership and management skills'. A 1993 survey of major employers of MBA graduates rated interpersonal skills and leadership skills as two (out of the top three) of the most important skills that organisations look for in their staff (*The Times*, February 1993).

At a general level, local authorities have consistently prided themselves on being 'good employers', yet closer examination of the elements that underlie the idea of a good employer sometimes suggest that, both in general and in particular authorities, many elements of the employment relationship are actually quite poor. One shire district council commissioned a study of the organisation as seen externally and by those who work within it. The impression gained from employee comments was not encouraging.

> at all levels employees report a lack of clear guidelines, absence of praise and no reward for achievement . . . it is felt that good work is taken for granted . . . promotion practice appears to be unfair, not on the basis of ability but the principle of 'if your face fits'. . . people who have a good interview technique get on, as do people who are cunning enough to choose higher profile work. . .
>
> There is no systematic appraisal of employees' performance or potential. Staff report no incentives to do a good job and a widespread acceptance of low standards' (unpublished report, district council, 1989).

This chapter examines the reasons why effective management of people is important for local authorities, it reviews some specific examples of the way in which local authorities are addressing this need, and considers the implications for individual managers of thinking about how effectively to manage people.

Why are people important?

Getting the management of people right is important to local government because, to an ever-increasing degree, the value and quality of services provided is dependent upon the people who work within the organisation. In the early years of local government development, the balance of expenditure was often on capital and infrastructural services – roads, water and drainage. Now, while still significant, these services represent a relatively low proportion of overall local government expenditure. In major authorities the personal services represent the largest proportion of expenditure and, in subjective terms, expenditure on staff represents the largest single element of the budget in virtually all local authorities.

In one financial year the largest local authority in the UK (Strathclyde) spent 57 per cent of its budget on employees, and the smallest local authority (Nairn), 65 per cent (Strathclyde and

Nairn Annual reports, 1991/1992). The effective contribution that people make to the work of an organisation can be judged at an everyday level. When staff within local authorities make a comparison between their own and other local authorities, they often refer to the balance of relationships between the people who work there. They will not assess a potential employer on the quality of the staff canteen, nor are they generally able to do so on the basis of comparing salaries and seeing the potential to earn a significantly greater salary elsewhere. The comparison, and perhaps the choice to move job, will usually be made on the basis of career opportunities and, the quality of the management; sometimes as a generalised and often unspecific view of whether that council is a 'good place to work'.

However, in practical terms, we often find that the actual practice is poor. Various reports on training in Britain demonstrate graphically and clearly how weak is our support for training and development at all levels within many sectors of British industry. This is despite the growing body of evidence that investment in and support for staff development and training can provide a considerable return for the employer's organisation. The report on the winners of the National Training Awards 1992 (National Training Awards, 1993) give examples of performance improvement through investment in staff development and training. The ambulance service in Dorset introduced paramedic training for all staff, an innovation which led to improved morale, reduced sickness among staff and lifesaving benefits for patients. The ground maintenance Direct Service Organisation (DSO) in the London Borough of Havering (the one local authority winner amongst eighty-one) developed a training programme for all staff involving multi-skilling, and management training. It won a contract bid against multinational rivals by a wide margin, improved staff turnover and absenteeism levels and turned round loss-making on the plant nursery. All the examples given in such a report indicate how, in facing a major change in the organisation, support for and investment in staff can be a substantial element in addressing that change.

The need for local authorities to work in a fast-changing environment requires many organisational and procedural changes which are often obvious, though far from simple to achieve. It also requires a change of culture and senior management attitude. If the changes simply mean restructuring, creating a different range of responsibilities, and creating different procedures and practices at the organisational level, then that change will not be enough. All of the environmental demands which are increasingly being placed on local authorities are of a kind that require decision-making to be devolved, responsibilities to be more broadly shared throughout the organisation, and of a type which involves staff who are nearer the 'front end' of the organisation in assuming greater responsibilities for service delivery and decisions than they have in the past. Simply to change procedures alone is not enough: the staff who are expected to operate with those new procedures must be encouraged, supported, and exhorted to do so. The extent to which this is happening varies from council to council, but telling observations have been made in various surveys that have examined public reaction to local government services both at national and local level. It is a frequently reported observation from such studies that the public often find local government staff 'very helpful', but in most cases a significant proportion of respondents indicate that the problem or question they raised with the local authority was 'not dealt with effectively' (National Consumer Council and Mori, 1991).

We can look beyond the survey data available in such authorities and examine why this kind of pattern is common in many areas of local government. It would appear that, in many cases, staff have habitually been conditioned to work on the basis of long-established systems and procedures which specify appropriate responses to a limited range of predetermined circumstances. Whenever circumstances do not appear to trigger a clear and preordained response then there is a tendency for decisions to be passed further up – in some cases to the top of – the organisation. That was perhaps appropriate for local government when the circumstances of individual and social choice were more limited, and when patterns of social behaviour were more regulated and predictable. As society has changed, so people expect those institutions which they deal with regularly to change and adapt to suit their circumstances. Put simply: we expect more choice as individuals and family units, and we get that choice from some organisations. We expect local government to respond in the same way. The crucial factor is the ability, willingness, and encouragement for staff to use initiative to respond positively to individual circumstance, and on occasion to take risks in acknowledging that diversity.

The effective development and management of staff within an organisation is a major factor in responding to competitive pressures and providing higher levels of service. A government-sponsored survey of training activities has suggested that, for the majority of employers, an increase in staff and management training was related to the demands of competitiveness and the improvement of customer service (Deloitte Haskins and Sells, 1989). Numerous examples of this are given in the reports of the National Training Awards for 1992. The critical consideration here for local government is the extent to which policies agreed centrally, in committee or at the corporate centre of the organisation, require the commitment of individual staff to be put into effective practice at an operational or public level. Recent observation of the implementation of equal opportunities policies in some local authorities would suggests there is often a considerable gap between policy exhortation and practical implementation (Kerley, 1993b).

There is a powerful contrast here between the practice of large commercial organisations and that of many local authorities. We all anticipate that in certain key areas of activity – simple correspondence, goods returned, sales practice – large commercial organisations will pursue a common and consistent practice on a multi-site basis across all branches. Many local authorities sometimes appear unable to achieve this on a single site and multi-departmental basis. So, for example, in many authorities we can find a considerable diversity of practice in replying to letters, style of correspondence, the expectation of how quickly the organisation will respond to a public contact. At the root of this comparison are many and complex factors. One of those which may be significant is the way in which staff are viewed as being recruited to and working within a professional and departmental setting, rather than perceiving themselves as working for 'the council' and serving the public. In a changing environment, local authorities are themselves forced to change in a way that will increasingly equip staff to serve the public. Tayside Regional Council (1990, p. 8), in their strategic management framework, state that one of their principal aims is to: 'Give staff the tools to do the job'. A central element in this process of giving the staff the tools and in providing an effective service to the public is the role of the manager as somebody who is responsible for managing people, a responsibility that has in the past sometimes been denied or subverted.

The impact of the manager

There have been numerous observations, studies and commentaries about what a manager does. The recent and increasing interest in the competence of managers within British industry has led to a more systematic analysis of the different roles and functions of a manager. In the first issue of the newsletter *Competences* the Local Government Management Board (1992) has described the process: 'Thousands of jobs across many sectors of industry and commerce in both the public and private sectors have been analysed to identify the areas of work executed by managers throughout the U.K. The standards defined the levels of performance to which U.K. managers and supervisors should aspire.' Fowler (1988) has commented on the tendency for discussion of management to either emphasise 'general' management or to concentrate on the functional specialisms – finance, marketing, personnel – into which management is often conveniently subdivided. He argues that this process has created considerable limitations, both for the understanding of what managers do, and for their own understanding of their responsibility for managing people within the organisation. 'The effective management of people is a central function of all managers so that effective personnel management is neither more nor less than effective general management' (p. vi).

It seems clear that local authorities now view the management of people as a significant responsibility for managerial staff. The London Borough of Ealing (1992) has produced a Management Development Strategy which identified appropriate core competences for managers within the borough. They were listed as: 'organising people and resources, managing people and developing them, communicating and networking' and the list continued through a range of other competences. An examination of recruitment advertisements for posts in local government (*Guardian*, February 1992) emphasises the importance attached to the management of people. 'proven skills in leadership and staff motivation' (area family services manager); 'a track record of achievement, and the ability to motivate and support staff through key changes' (community social services manager). A survey by the PA consulting the *Local Government Chronicle* (1990) suggested that among the different types of local authorities, 'managing people' was the subject of coordinated management development programmes on the part of the greatest number of councils. The same survey also showed considerable emphasis on communications skills, team building and appraising as part of local authority management development programmes.

The paradox of managing people

At the heart of the apparent emphasis on managing people in local government there is a paradox. In effect, managers in local government have both been denied, and have themselves avoided, many of the central elements of a responsibility for managing people. There are various aspects of the management of people: appointment, dismissal, day-to-day supervision, appraisal and development, encouragement, motivation and reward. The list could be extended, but the point of particular significance in this context is that, for the typical manager in local government, responsibility for these various elements of managing people is at best shared, and at worst denied.

Appointments are typically made by a panel, on which the manager may or may not be a member but in any event will not usually have a veto. Dismissal may be the responsibility of a line manager but, even outside the limits of statutory protection enjoyed by employees, there are in most councils additional internal and external appeal procedures where such a decision can be reconsidered and may be overturned or amended. Day-to-day discipline is often mediated by a requirement to observe consistent procedures throughout the organisation and to involve central personnel staff in the disciplinary process. Whilst it may be within the individual manager's abilities and understanding to motivate and encourage staff, it is often not possible for immediate and relatively minor local decisions to change the reward pattern of a group of employees within the council. Processes and decisions at the centre of the organisation are concerned to ensure apparent consistency, which is too frequently interpreted as taking no actions which will disturb the status quo.

It is clear that in publicly accountable and democratically controlled organisations there must be constraints upon the individual to prevent him or her making arbitrary, capricious and inconsistent decisions. However, such constraining arrangements, which are commonly found in many local authorities, have tended to create a climate which can militate against the effective management of people within the organisation. A manager can deny the responsibility for a subordinates performance on the grounds that he or she was not responsible for the appointment – somebody else made it. Another manager can create a climate where effective disciplinary sanctions are rare, on the basis that 'if I discipline, members will just overturn it anyway'. The consequences of this for the effective management of people can be seen in many local authority contexts.

A report on management training for promoted social workers in the London borough of Islington (Gilbert, 1992, p. 28) described the fears of newly appointed managers in social services: 'often they are unsure about taking up a management role . . . especially in terms of getting on with colleagues with whom they have been part of a team. Feeling comfortable with the power is a big issue. It is not really part of social services culture.' Those taking up such management positions apparently revealed a number of common fears; these included

- that a member of their staff will refuse to accept their authority.
- that by managing people they will abuse or hurt them in some way.
- the power dynamics and the supervisory role, for example, if the other person is older, different race or gender, or used to be their peer.
- managers will not be able to deal effectively with people who are not up to the mark.

Research carried out for this book among managers in different Scottish local authorities would suggest that operational managers in local government have themselves assumed a limited view of the range of their responsibilities for managing people (Kerley, 1993c). Two groups of managers, one drawn from staff in a variety of settings within a large regional council, the other covering a variety of responsibilities and a mixture of island, district and regional councils, were asked about their perception of the roles they fulfilled as a manager. In particular they were asked to indicate the range of roles which they were conscious of most frequently doing, and as a contrast the range of roles which they least frequently found themselves doing. Figure 4.1 indicates the 'most important' and 'least frequent' of the roles they indicate which relate to the management of people.

What these responses suggest is that two typical groups of managers see themselves as having authority over staff, yet little responsibility for those areas of people management – development and appraisal – which are in some ways the most challenging and difficult aspects of the people management role. In effect, what is suggested here is a double paradox for a typical manager in local government. This person is expected by the organisation to have a major responsibility for managing people. However, he or she is also denied by the organisation many of the tools which are necessary and important components in the process of managing people. Perhaps as a consequence of this, the typical manager often shies away from critical elements of that management task. Ironically, in doing so such managers are compounding the problem, because they are denying themselves methods and approaches which can be very important elements in the effective managing of people. Some of the ways in which the individual manager can retrieve this position are discussed later in this chapter. Before considering the courses of action open to individual managers it is important to examine some of the changing trends observable in the broader pattern of personnel management within local government.

FIGURE 4.1   The different roles of the managers

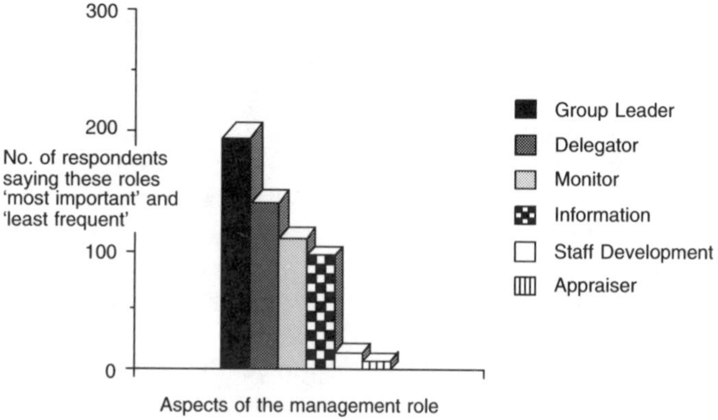

Sources: Kerley 1993: questionnaire data.

The changing personnel environment

The changes occurring in the working environment of local government and the manner in which local government is organising itself to meet those changes is resulting in a complex and often contradictory pattern of change and development relating to the management of staff. These changes have been necessary as local government has adjusted to a changing world. In a typically crisp fashion the Audit Commission for England and Wales described the reasons why local government was having to focus far more on the management of people:

> Local government is a people business. Many of the worst problems faced by authorities today result from the absence of good people, or poor training or motivation of those people who remain. In part, at least, this is a self inflicted wound. Some authorities have neglected personnel management, and their responsibility to train and retain a skilled work force (Audit Commission, 1988a, p. 4).

In a subsequent management paper entitled *People Management: Human Resources in Tomorrow's Public Services* (Audit Commission, 1991) it was suggested that the traditional approach to personnel management in local government was characterised by a number of interlinked features. Many local authorities had developed a highly centralised control of staffing numbers, grading and structures, enforced through detailed rules and regulations that extended across all departments and grades. There was often little structured attempt at forward planning for developing the appropriate skills mix. Recruitment followed an often predictable pattern, with an overemphasis on either internal or external appointment and little consideration of the appropriate forms of recruitment for different parts of the organisation. Many councils were almost totally reliant on nationalised and centralised negotiation for wage and salary agreements and conditions of services.

In all of this traditional pattern we find yet another paradox about the employment relationship within local government. Local government is sometimes described as one of the biggest employers in our society, yet it is not: it is actually several hundred different employers with their own local needs and requirements. Yet simultaneously for many years individual local authorities voluntarily handed a large element of their employment responsibilities over to weakly representative national organisations, the decisions of which would often be the subject of complaint by individual members and individual councils. Such arrangements were seen at their most exaggerated during periods of statutory pay policy in the 1960s and 1970s, when decisions on grading, regrading and the relative pay levels between different groups of staff in different councils were often decided by a small group of officials policing national pay structures from the headquarters of the national employers' organisation.

During the 1980s and into the early 1990s there have been considerable changes in this traditional postwar pattern of local government personnel management. The implications and consequences of some such changes – with, for example, a minority of local authorities opting for localised pay-bargaining – have been controversial, and the consequences have been mixed. Increasing numbers of local authorities are seeing a consistent pattern of change, in which a renewed emphasis on dynamic personnel management is becoming very significant in the management of the authority.

The recent Local Government Management Board study of *The Well Managed Authority* (1993, p. 2) has suggested that one of the central features of a well-managed authority has been an effective integration of the values and culture of the authority with an appropriate strategy, delivered through the right systems and using staff in a creative fashion, 'aimed at optimising the collective (and individual) contributions of employees, and dealing both with communicating the authorities values, vision, strategy etc: and with motivating staff to high performance.' Individual local authorities have taken account of the implications of these changes in reviewing their approach to personnel management. For example, Gloucestershire County Council 'has adopted a policy of devolution into departments on more day-to-day aspects of the personnel function' (Gloucestershire County Council, 1989, p. 1).

The reliance on procedure

Characteristic of personnel practice in many large organisations, including local authorities, is an often over-reliance on an array of discrete procedures. The weakness of such an approach is that such procedures, whilst clearly interrelated in their impact upon individuals, the work group and the organisation, are often not effectively integrated. This is despite a recognition at strategic level that the process of integration is vitally necessary. A codicil to the policy documents from Gloucestershire County Council makes this point:

'Necessarily for the purposes of readily summarising the range of personnel management services and there monitoring, this Code is divided into sections. It is recognised, however, that the success of the total personnel function rests on the provision of a fully integrated approach to the delivery of services' (Gloucestershire County Council, 1989, p. 12). This is an important point, because it appears that an increasing proportion of public service organisations have instituted formal systems for dealing with different aspects of the employment relationship during the 1980s. One survey (Industrial Relations Review Report, 1992, p. 9) shows that, over the period 1980–90, the proportion of respondents reporting the introduction of formalised systems for discipline has increased from 83 per cent to 98 per cent; and those dealing with dismissal from 83 per cent to 96 per cent. At an organisational level this may suggest that such organisations, including many local authorities, are not creating the most appropriate climate to manage in the way their rhetoric and aspiration suggest they wish to be managed; they are not equipping and supporting their managers to manage in the way that public statements and job advertisements suggest they wish them to. Scase (1991) has suggested that this may be a phenomenon which is widespread in British industry:

The 'New Organisation' demands leadership through inspiration, motivation and commitment rather than management by memos from behind closed doors . . . instead of managing through rules and formal procedures within hierarchies, sophisticated interpersonal skills are needed . . . the training of managers in Britain emphasises the need for specialist technical skills to the neglect of 'intangible' 'soft' human resource skills.

The consequence of this pattern is that the organisation itself creates a climate and a working environment in which the manager is encouraged not to think creatively about the people for whom he or she is responsible but instead to view them through a prism of

systems and procedures which do not encourage any clear view of
the inter-relationship between different aspects of the employment
relationship.

Figure 4.2 illustrates some of the many complex aspects of the
management of people, and attempts to suggest the relationship
between them for the individual, for the work group, and for the
organisation as a whole. The manager must understand that action
upon any one of these areas has implications for other elements,
which are held in a delicate balance. The figure will suggest to
readers some of the many linkages that can be observed, so one
example will serve as an illustration. Increasing numbers of local
authorities are now introducing formal systems of staff and management appraisal within the council. Frequently – and understandably
– it is often emphasised that this is a process which should be being
seen as being quite distinct from any disciplinary or other procedures within the organisation. Such approaches to appraisal often
state that appraisal is unrelated to promotion or appointment within

FIGURE 4.2   Managing people: the individual and the group

the organisation. Formally correct, but little consideration is given to the possibility that the manager will be forced to think about staff and examine their working patterns and performance in ways that will influence subsequent judgements in disciplinary and promotion matters. Ironically, the individual appraised is under no such inhibition; if he or she is subsequently subject to disciplinary procedures or a candidate for promotion it is of course always possible to introduce *favourable* appraisal records into either process – yet few authorities appear to have given any consideration to the possibility of this occurring or the likely consequences.

Action by the manager

Many limitations and constraints are therefore placed upon the individual manager by institutional procedure. None-the-less, there are still numerous opportunities available to him or her to influence and affect the way in which staff are managed and motivated. To do this the manager will have to take a far more proactive view of the relationship with staff, and develop a strategy for the more dynamic management of people.

There are a number of aspects of this process which demand an approach to managing people which differ from that usually seen within the typical organisation. This is not difficult, but it does require some effort and imagination:

● An effective manager will need to devote more effort and imagination to build up a better understanding of the staff who are working for him or her. We may think that we know the people who work for us, but often our views about them are formed on the basis of informal and impressionistic evidence, without any clear examination of what motivates them or what career ambitions they have. One study of appraisal in a Scottish local authority showed that even among the most senior staff in the directorate of one department, some 80 per cent of those responsible for appraising their immediate subordinates discovered things about them they 'did not know before' a formal appraisal interview had taken place (Kerley, 1993c). Assumptions made about staff will often colour staffing decisions without the benefit of a direct and open discussion with the people involved. It may be appropriate for a manager to conduct a formal staff development audit among those people who work within the unit or section. This can be done on a less formal basis, but certainly it will require a more rigorous analysis of staff motivation and interests than occurs in many organisational settings.

- An effective manager will encourage self-development among staff. The good manager should not be afraid of those subordinates who are keen to do part of the manager's job or may even be able to do part of the job better than he or she can. In a previous chapter it was suggested that an effective manager is continuously checking that the work in which he or she is involved is sufficiently demanding to provide for effective career development. The corollary of this is that the work is released which subordinates can grow and develop into. All large organisations have a tendency to suppress talent and ability. The common message which many such organisations give – either explicitly or implicitly – says, in effect, 'this is a job for somebody on PO15. You are only on PO14: you can't do it.' An effective manager will reject that proposition, will encourage staff to believe they can do something, and will find ways to press the organisation to allow them to do that work.

- Delegation of responsibility and duty is too often seen as an almost mechanical process. Tasks are defined, objectives are decided upon, the most appropriate person for the task is found, and the work is delegated with reporting through exception or on completion. All too often the assumption is made that the most appropriate person for the job is the one who can 'do it best' or 'always deliver'. Many managers do not consider the process of delegation as encouraging and developing effective performance among their staff. It is a useful occasional exercise for a manager to stop and examine the manner in which work is delegated within the organisation. This may be through the formal delegation of particular tasks and activities: a project or a committee report. It may be the involvement of members of staff in working parties or interdisciplinary and interdepartmental groups of one kind or another. All are in their way different forms of delegation of a task, responsibility or opportunity. What sometimes emerges on closer examination of this process will often suggest that a tendency is to concentrate such choices on a limited range of people. A manager who is responsible for perhaps ten or twelve people with roughly the same basic responsibilities and experience will, on examination, often find that the choice of persons to whom such tasks and activities are delegated is perhaps limited to two or three out of the ten or twelve. The important point is that this is often *not* intentional; indeed, quite the opposite – it is unintentional and often unconsidered. Despite this it gives a very clear message to both groups of people, the chosen and the not chosen. The performance of the former group is reinforced because they see themselves as doing well; the performance of the latter group is reinforced negatively, because they see themselves as not judged capable of exercising effective performance. It is an easy exercise for any manger to carry out this analysis; simply examine your practice over the past six months or year. If you find this kind of pattern in your decisions on delegation, then think hard about why such a pattern has emerged and how you may begin to redress this discriminatory balance.

- A good manager will use the opportunities for training and development available within the organisation in a positive and proactive way. In many local authorities it is clearly still the case that an involvement in training is related to an ad hoc expression of interest in a catalogue of training courses that is circulated routinely around the unit or department. If a member of staff is available to go, if the unit has any funds available, if the material is received in time, then a name may be put forward. If too many names are put forward or if not enough money is available then an arbitrary choice of nomination will be made, either by a senior member of staff or even perhaps by somebody with no line management responsibility for the group of people involved.

This process of staff development can – and should – be handled differently by the effective manager who is assuming the management responsibility for the development of his or her staff. They should not be allowed to default into or out of the training opportunities available at a particular time. More appropriately, the manager concerned should be making clear choices about staff development based upon a broader view of the development needs of the individual and the organisation. And those development needs should be integrated with both experience and potential opportunities within the working environment. There should be a far closer relationship between off-the-job training and on-the-job experience, so that both effectively reinforce each other and reinforce the process of learning that should be a constant feature of the effective management of people.

Some points for discussion

1. What characterises a 'good employer'?
2. Are local authorities 'good employers'?
3. Has your background and training equipped you to be a good manager of people?
4. How conscious are you of the way in which you delegate tasks and activities to staff?
5. How much time do you commit to encouraging staff development?

5 Managing Finance

The organisation and control of council finances is central to the management of an authority. Notwithstanding various other aspects of the planning and decision-making process, the budget represents the most concrete and explicit statement of what the organisation hopes to do and achieve in current and future years; it is a quantitative expression of the plans of the organisation. It also provides a very revealing indication of the actual priorities of the organisation, and the reality that underlies – and may sometimes deny – the public statements of purpose and objectives. A comment made on the management of central government applies equally to local authorities throughout the country: 'the task of allocating money is the most pervasive and informative operation of governmentn. . . . In short, the expenditure process is an immense window into the reality of British political administration' (Heclo and Wildavsky, 1991, p. xii). Budgets and financing are therefore important to any organisation; they are particularly important to public organisations. This is because a local authority is spending public money, the majority of which is raised through taxation of one form or another, and therefore it must be accountable for the expenditure of this money. Budgets are also important because they are based upon an appropriation of funds from the taxpayer, rather than any projection of income which the organisation can raise from the sale of goods or services to willing customers. An understanding of budgets and finance is important for managers in local government, as is observed in a publication by the Chartered Institute of Public Finance and Accounting (CIPFA): 'finance is the common currency for all local government services in determining the scale on which they are to be carried out, both in absolute terms and in relation of one to another' (CIPFA, 1990, p. 1).

Unfortunately, an understanding of local government finance, and the development of the necessary management skills to handle effectively the financial responsibilities which may rest with an individual manager, has been hampered by the mystique that is often seen to surround local government financing. The authors of a recent 'Guide to local government finance' (Local Government Information Unit, 1993) comment that :

> There is mystery surrounding the financing of local government. Few people understand how the system really works, yet millions are affected by it . . . As with many 'technical' subjects, often those who understand its complications are the least able to explain it in simple terms. They are too close to the subject; too concerned that omitting one single detail will give the wrong impression . . . there are also those with a vested interest in keeping the system mysterious (p. 5).

That sense of 'mystery' can be observed in many different local government settings and in many different authorities. At a national level, the continuing efforts of various governments to limit and constrain local government expenditure has led to a financial system of fantastic and almost incomprehensible complexity. As that complexity has increased over time, the capacity of even central government effectively to influence levels of local government spending in a predictable way has become very limited. In his autobiography, the Secretary of State responsible for introducing the community charge comments that at the time of introduction he thought that the typical community charge 'would work out on average at about £200 per head . . . but it didn't; it worked out at nearer £400'. He rather wistfully commented, 'I have never quite understood why the first years community charge came out in practice quite so much higher than we expected when we fixed the grant level in July 89' (Ridley, 1992, pp. 130–1) The complexity of central government financial support for local government has confused rather than clarified an understanding of local government finance.

At the level of the individual council, while some authorities attempt to follow a budget process which maximises the level of participation by senior staff and members, there are still many where budget decisions are made in effect by a very limited circle of senior members supported by a handful of senior officials. One major study of local government budgeting describes the practice in several authorities where such groupings are variously described as 'The star chamber'; 'The gang of four'; and 'The big three' (Elcock *et al.*, 1989, p. 90). This longstanding tradition of central control and direction of local authority financing, compounded by centralisation within the council, has itself created over time a perception among even relatively senior staff in local authorities that on financial matters they are subordinate to a small handful of central officials. This has discouraged them or, at worst, disabled them from taking any interest in financial matters. Only a few years ago, during a discussion with the head of a large department within one district council, a direct question about financial management and budgetary control within the department met the response 'I just keep spending money until the director of finance tells me to stop' (private interview). Whilst this answer may exaggerate somewhat flippantly, the underlying attitude and approach that it suggests is not too far removed from the kind of arrangement found in many local authorities until quite recently.

We must recognise however that the traditional approach, which firmly places control of the budget and of financing in the hands of the financial centre of the organisation, is changing. For various reasons, departmental and service managers are taking an increasing interest in, and attempting to develop a greater control over, the financing of their functions and activities within the organisation. One factor in this has been the post-reorganisation shift to a more council-wide and corporate form of management. It has created in many councils a layer of senior officials who wish to take an overview of the workings of the authority and therefore need to understand the financial management of the authority. In interview, one chief executive described how 'I really had to struggle to understand the finance of it but I knew that was vital to getting a grip on the organisation' (district council chief executive). In effect, this is a recognition that if managers are to be effective and accountable then they cannot alienate themselves from influence over and control of any part of the resources of the organisation. They must necessarily understand and grapple with the financing of their service, just as they must take a responsibility for the management of that other resource – people.

The impact of this continuing change can be seen in various local authorities and in a number of ways. At the most basic level, many local authority training programmes now attempt to develop an understanding of 'finance for non-financial managers' in courses which, for example, are intended for: 'Senior and middle managers who direct and control budgets. Professional staff with a need for

understanding of financial decision-making and control processes
. . . this course allows managers to build on their basic knowledge
and to gain a better understanding of the financial concepts within
local authorities and the private sector which drive management
decisions' (Lothian Regional Council, 1993, p. 32).

Elsewhere in many local authorities there is increased incidence of
finance staff moving into senior management positions within
service departments. The service department are clearly recognising
a need to have financial expertise at a senior level which will see itself
more allied to the needs of the service department than of the central
control function. This is in marked contrast to the previous practice
of many authorities, where any financial expertise at the periphery –
i.e. in service departments – was often less effective than the
financial expertise at the centre. This chapter attempts to consider
some of the reasons why local government managers are steadily
finding themselves required to assume a greater responsibility for
financial matters. It also considers what those managers need to
know in order to do this, and what skills they need to develop. It
touches upon some of the changes within the authority which those
managers – if they are to be effective – will have to obtain. There is
no attempt here to discuss the broader process of financing local
government: there are several books which do this, and all provide
important background reading for an understanding of that process.

The financial function in local government

The financial function has always been important to the operation
of local government. A 'proper financial officer' is the one appointment explicitly required of all local authorities; there is no comparable requirement to appoint a chief executive. Prior to the
reorganisation of local government in the early 1970s, and the
creation in most authorities of a policy and resources committee,
the finance committee was often the most important committee in
the council. Directors of finance will often – only half jokingly –
refer to themselves as 'the abominable No man'. Preparation of a
budget, agreement of a budget – and in recent years in some councils
the revision of a budget at mid-year – are among the most important
features in a local authority year, irresistibly driving all other aspects

of the planning cycle to one side. The longstanding place of finance at the centre of local government activity has both created and been sustained by a legacy of traditional arrangements, some of which – it would be argued – have militated against the more effective operation of the authority.

The dominant characteristic of local authority financial management is still an emphasis on *financial* accounting; that is, a form of accounting derived from the traditional 'stewardship function'. This can be contrasted with the more action-orientated processes of *management* accounting; which is essentially concerned with the provision and use of information for management purposes, which helps to develop policies, long- and short-term planning, controls the activities of the organisation, chooses between alternatives, and appraises investment decisions and operations. Clearly it would be an exaggeration to suggest that local authority financial management is entirely concerned with financial accounting, but many of the features of that process and much of the practice indicates just how important that component is. Consider some aspects of this. Until quite recently, many local authority financial systems were geared to fulfilling the interests of the financial centre rather than the everyday requirements of the operational manager. Enormous effort and resources are invested in producing an annual report and statement of accounts – indeed, crueller critics would suggest that many of the financial systems are *principally* geared towards producing that statement of accounts. As one local authority manager observed in interview 'I want to generate accurate immediate figures; the finance department is concerned with history' (social work manager). The financial practices of many councils emphasise legality and probity rather than the effective use of resources. As Tomkins (1987, p. 63) observes in connection with central government: 'probity and legality is also strongly entrenched . . . A "circle of accountability" was established. The system was, despite some claims by the Exchequer and Audit Department to have conducted broader efficiency and effectiveness audits for years, *essentially* designed to check on probity and compliance with appropriations.' A similar observation can be made about practice in local government. Until comparatively recently the concern of both internal and external auditors was for legality and probity, and only in recent years have the auditors concerned themselves with effectiveness and 'value for money' work.

It is of course arguable that one of the reasons why there is little corruption and misappropriation in British local government is precisely because of this emphasis on probity, but we might equally suggest that there are other social and cultural reasons which make such illegal activity less likely in this country than in some other. That emphasis on probity is in itself a longstanding tradition, and one that both encourages and reinforces the comfort element that is a dominant value in the accounting practices of local government. The influence of historical tradition on local government accounting practices is reflected in one of the most rigidly imposed forms of procedure, the emphasis on 'annuality'. This practice, imposed still in many councils, states that the budget vote is for the current financial year, and that any money not spent by the end of the financial year is lost to that particular unit and called into the central reserves of the authority. As Aneurin Bevan rightly observed, this process, which he described as a 'pastoral' tradition, owes much to the annual harvest cycle. More harshly, Knight (1983) refers to this as a 'mediaeval practice'. It is a practice which sees many responsible budget-holders during February and March each year spending time and money on ordering trivial and inessential items, or finding some way to circumvent procedures imposed by the finance department. It is of course a calculation that is impossible to make, but if on average each responsible budget-holder in local government was spending just £500 in this way, the total involved would outweigh the amount of loss to local government through fraudulent and corrupt practices many times over.

Another significant feature of local authority accounting is the emphasis it has traditionally given to central control. This is reflected in the plethora of forms and procedures often necessary for the commitment of any funds, but also in the degree to which the central finance function has attempted to exert control over – and in effect often to second-guess – those responsible for spending in service departments. This practice is now in decline in many authorities as responsibility for managing resources is increasingly devolved, but there is still a tension there which is particularly exacerbated when the authority needs to make cuts in its budget. This occurs both during the period of budget setting and (in an increasing number of authorities) when, after the budget has been set, it becomes necessary to adjust it because of government intervention. The central control therefore can take different forms. Game (1987) describes the final decisions on a budget in Birmingham which is typical of the pattern in many authorities:

> So, after weeks of attempted prioritisation and careful calcula-tion, some of the most critical allocation decisions were actually taken quite literally at the eleventh hour in a 'short, sharp round the table exercise': right, we'll have a million and a half off education, half a million off social services, so much off con-sumer protection and so on – that's how it was finally done (p. 64).

This process is brutal, bloody, and essentially asserts the power of the centre, which is concerned with meeting government guidelines or ensuring that the increase in the rate/community charge/council tax is kept low. Those at the centre exert this power over the staff in service departments who have planned and proposed and evaluated various options over time. The mid-year intervention more usually takes the form of an edict to reduce mileage travelled, slow down on filling staff vacancies, reduce peak-rate telephone calls and so on. Both processes indicate the strength of the centre, and its unwill-ingness to trust those people to whom it delegates the notional responsibility for managing services. It also partly of course reflects the fact that until very recently in many councils, and even today in others, management information systems are so poor that the only way in which the organisation can ensure compliance with the central policy decision is unilaterally to reduce expenditure, as though putting a spoke in the front wheel of a bicycle.

It is of course unfair and a caricature to imply that all those who work in local authority finance are unreconstructed traditionalists ever keen to assert their authority and control over irresponsible service departments. That traditional relationship worked, in its time, because it suited the circumstances of the time. As times change, so the finance department, the members and the managers in the service departments need to create a new working relationship that will reflect changed circumstances within the council. Before we consider what skills and knowledge of financial management need to be extended within the council, we need first of all to consider who exactly manages the money within a local authority on a day-to-day basis.

Who does manage the money?

Setting the budget

The statutory requirement to set a budget and agree the level of
council tax rests with a meeting of the full council. Indeed, it is one
of the few decisions which a local authority cannot delegate to any
officer or committee. Observation of many authorities makes it
quite clear that, while the formal process requires the decision to be
made in this way, unless the council is 'hung', actual decisions on
setting budget are made by the majority group, more probably, by a
relatively small group of elite members in that group, or a small core
of leading members in 'independent' councils. The process of
discussion, bargaining, trading and decision-making that leads to
the presentation of a suggested final budget is a complex and lengthy
exercise in even the smallest of councils. It is a process that, in the
more politically organised and majority-controlled councils, usually
involves bilateral discussion between committee convener and chief
officer, parallelled by discussion among chief officers and the
submission of conclusions to a relatively small budget group of
leading members, often supplemented by the most senior officials of
the council, with councillors and officials working very closely
together in an informal exercise of joint control.

As the observation of practice in Birmingham cited above will
suggest, the final stages of this decision-making process may be
confused and messy. The ever-present demand to expand services
and therefore to spend more money must be reconciled with the often
pressing – and sometimes imposed – requirement to limit the increase
in local taxation and expenditure. If it comes to a crunch the latter
pressure prevails, and decisions are made often on an arbitrary and
ill-informed basis to take proposals out of the budget that may have
been the subject of extensive planning, preparation and consultation
at departmental level. In their review of budget-setting in local
government Elcock *et al.* (1989) even cite one instance of members
making decisions 'on the basis of a mis- interpretation of the officers'
proposals . . . to a policy of making pro-rata cuts in each committees
estimates, instead of . . . shifting resources to the social services
committee and away from the education committee' (pp. 65–6).
Figure 5.1 shows a simplified model of the budget decision-making
process in Strathclyde Region in the early 1990s.

FIGURE 5.1 The corporate budget cycle

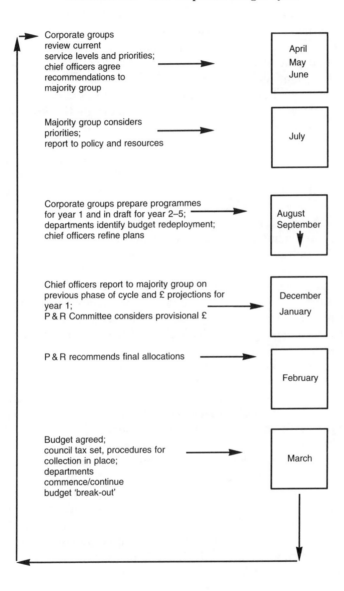

Flexibility and budgetary discretion

To a far greater extent than is sometimes realised, when current members make a final decision on the local authority budget, influenced by government constraint and financial support, a very substantial part of the budget for many local authorities was in effect decided by those serving as officers and councillors more than thirty years ago. Levels of service provision and levels of expenditure in many local authorities today owe far more to the historical baseline which current councils inherited than is sometimes apparent. Levels of financial support from central government, and the mechanisms of restraint which that government has attempted to place on councils, have generally acted to place limitations on those councils which have historically spent at low levels. The consequence of this is that where political control or political ideas have changed in recent years it has proved difficult for those councils to bring up levels of expenditure to match those of historically high-spending councils. In Lothian Region, for example, of the almost fifty secondary schools, fewer than 10 per cent have actually been built in the near two decades since the reorganisation of local government. In most councils, the pattern of service provision, and the range of facilities and budget levels, are to a great extent historically given rather than determined afresh by councils working from a clean sheet.

Some councils have attempted a complete review of budget provision – sometimes called zero-based budgeting – but this has usually been abandoned as being excessively complex and demanding of both time and energy for members and officers. The consequence of this is that the typical budget for a department and the budget for individual institutions or units within the department will actually provide very little scope for discretionary expenditure by a manager. The degree of discretion will, by its nature vary from service to service and council to council, but a range of perhaps 1 to 3 per cent per annum of 'free monies' would perhaps be typical. It may of course be open to individual managers to attempt to increase their degree of discretion by building unspecified amounts into their financial plans to give them more freedom. The Local Government Information Unit (1993, p. 61) reprint an extract from a London borough budget summary which shows the total net provision in 1989/90 of £289,000 for the registration of electors. Many of the component elements are detailed to an almost fastidious degree: £100 for photocopying, £420 for travelling expenses and £5,200 for 'miscellaneous'. The original budget for 1990/91 shows an increase from £289,000 to £406,260. However, whilst the travelling expenses have been pared down to £120, and photocopying reduced to nil cost, the 'miscellaneous' figure has increased to £150,430 or almost 40 per cent of the total budget. The authors do not record whether these proposals were agreed when put to a committee.

The point to be noted is the degree to which managers of particular services usually see very little discretionary growth in their budget which is not in some way or another specified as being allocated to particular and often closely defined activities. In many councils there is now an increasing likelihood that departments will be given some limited authority to 'vire' monies from one budget head to another where they think it is appropriate to do so. Frequently, however, this requires adherence to a quite complex procedure which often involves a formal report to committee, and quite persuasive justification for transferring even comparatively small amounts.

Who spends the money?

It is not readily apparent from job title alone who, in any local authority, has any need or authority to spend money on behalf of the authority. Allied to that is the phenomenon whereby a member of staff may notionally be responsible for control of substantial amounts of money but actually has little discretion in how he or she spends it, and does so within closely defined parameters and constraints.

A very informal inquiry amongst four groups of senior staff in one large local authority suggested that responsibilities for financial management were not as widespread as might at first have been thought. Among four groups of between twelve and sixteen people, approximately half of those in each group had any financial management responsibility at all. Some of these people, for example an architect, might be responsible for a considerable number of staff and the supervision of a variety of projects but possess no authority to commit any expenditure or spend any money. Amongst those who did have some financial responsibilities, the nature of that financial responsibility varied quite considerably. An engineer would perhaps have overall supervisory responsibility for major materials purchases amounting to several million pounds in a year, but would do so within the confines of an agreed purchasing contract over which he or she had no control. The management requirement would be to place occasional orders for large bulk purchases of materials and ensure that over the course of a financial year purchases did not exceed budget.

In some respects, this pattern of financial management responsibility – or rather the absence of financial management responsibility – is perhaps characteristic of large-scale public service programmes. Metcalfe and Richards (1990) observe a similar phenomenon in the civil service, which was highlighted by the attempts under the Financial Management Initiative to improve efficiency and effectiveness in central government: 'The culture and traditions of Whitehall have not favoured strong line management. . . . Managers nominally responsible for a particular area of activity have had little real say in the resources allocated to them or very much flexibility in using them.' They add (ominously in the context): 'this was not fertile soil in which to try and cultivate positive attitudes to accountable management' (pp. 188–9).

The important contrast in local government is here between those managers who have notional financial management responsibility for large sums of money but are very fettered as to how it is spent, and those managers who have responsibilities for perhaps smaller amounts of money, with considerable discretion in its use, and little experience in how effectively to manage that. A social services area manager, for example, may have responsibility for funds that can be disbursed to clients; control over mileage and expense allowances for social work staff; discretion over allocating the hours of home helps; and control of overtime payments. In the majority of councils, he or she will still not have effective information and support systems for monitoring and controlling these budgets. Alternatively, a manager in arts or sports may be expected to promote activities, spend money on activities and exhibitions, purchase materials and displays. Such decisions will be taken in the context of a broader working environment – sports and the arts – where negotiation over price, quantity and informal agreements are the norm. Such arrangements do not fit well with the more circumscribed and formalised procedures of local government financial control.

Impressionistic evidence and observation would suggest that in the majority of cases where local authorities find they are required to take legal action over instances of fraud or theft, it usually involves relatively small amounts of money handled in an ad hoc and ill-organised manner which are therefore particularly susceptible to the temptation of access. If more managers in local government are to be expected to assume more responsibility for financial manage-ment, then councils need to give far more attention to what such managers need to know, the skills they need to acquire, and the powers they need to have in order to do their job effectively. The second half of this chapter moves on to consider these factors.

What do managers need to know (1)

To manage the finances of his or her unit or institution within the council effectively, a manager needs to have a general understanding of the broader context of local authority finance. The broad principle, rather than the technical detail, of the way in which the government guidelines and limits on expenditure are set, along with a general understanding of how the government determines the balance of external financing to different local authorities, is a necessary background for somebody in a position of responsibility within a council. So, for example, it is important for staff to understand that when the relevant minister indicates that local authorities should be spending more on a particular service there are in fact few mechanisms which ensure that this wish will translate through into the stage of implementation in the budget of any particular council. Such people will also need to be familiar with and have access to the basis documentation of authority-wide financial management – budget books and the annual report. Unless a manager is comfortable with handling those documents, and all the data and information that they contain, then the financial process will continue to be the 'mystery' that it still is for many.

The effective manager will also need to be aware of the budget timetable and budgetary processes within the individual council. He or she should be aware that a proposal which at present is at the stage of a bright idea will need to be worked up into a serious proposition with effective supporting detail and documentation by April or May of any year if it is even to be considered for inclusion in the financial plans for the following year. It also then becomes important to understand the particular features of that area of the authority's activities which are the responsibility of a particular manager. Is it a statutory function? Is it a regulatory function – the activity level of which is determined by other organisations and individuals (for example planning applications)? Is it an activity which is discretionary and can be dispensed with by the local authority? Is it an activity for which the authority levels charges – to businesses or individuals? If so, does the accountable manager have any influence on those charges or must any change in this area depend on a general council decision on the level of charges overall? If a manager is to engage actively with the decision-making process within the council, then he or she must establish answers to all these questions and clearly define the approach that should be taken, to intervene effectively in the broad process of budget decision-making. It is also necessary to establish who does what, who decides what, and how they decide in relation to the council and departmental budget. Do decision-makers reward those who suggest alternative ideas for activities and expenditure? Do they encourage the 'stand pat' approach to budget-making, which is occasionally varied through a central decision to make a pro rata increase or reduction on every budget head in every department of the council.

There are different approaches to budget allocation even within departments and units and it becomes important for each manager to understand how he or she is treated and, in turn, determine how the unit budget will be allocated. Knight (1983) discusses some possible strategies for finance allocation which will be readily recognised by those who work in many areas of local government. The first is benevolent despotism where, despite some consultation, the money is allocated on the decision of the senior manager, often to those who are artful and or favoured. Zero-basing attempts to evaluate budget proposals on their merit and against broader policies that may be appropriate to the council. A more frequently seen approach is that of creeping incrementalism, which simply adds a small proportion to the previous year's allocation based upon the general level of uplift or on the rate of inflation assumed by the council. Such an approach will have the advantage of not being painful for many people, but will entrench the existing allocations and programme – often to the point of ossification – and will not encourage new developments and activities. The formula approach uses a variety of data to attempt finance allocation on the basis of predefined criteria. The more complex the criteria – always a temptation – the more unpredictable will be the result. It can also encourage those involved in the process to seek constantly to vary the different data elements involved in order to try to enhance their particular position.

What is suggested in all of the above is that, whilst the individual manager will have no part in the overall budget decisions of the authority, it is important that he or she has an understanding of how such decisions are made and also an awareness of where there are opportunities to attempt an intervention in the decision-making process. Once that resolution has been made it then becomes important to consider what knowledge is needed to run the finances of the unit for which the manager is responsible.

What do managers need to know (2)

The performance budget system which Tayside Regional Council (1990) is introducing is typical of the kind of changes in financial management and responsibility which many local authorities are introducing. That proposes, among other things, to pass

> accountability to middle managers who *spend* the income and deliver services. It gets accountability there
> - by breaking the budget into 'cost centres' and giving individual managers responsibility for (one or more) cost centres
> - by requiring the managers to produce a statement of key results – the action plan
> - by requiring the managers to produce a statement of performance (how far key results achieved) at the end of year (p. 8).

If operational managers within any council are to demonstrate that degree of accountability and responsibility then they will need to develop a new understanding of a number of different elements of the way in which financial management operates within the council.

The most obvious and immediate requirement is that they will need to know the limits of their authority and discretion. This may seem so obvious as not to merit comment, but the traditional pattern of local authority decision-making has left many decisions to shared and consensual decision-making in a way which has acted to diffuse and confuse decision-making responsibilities.

With an increased tendency to disaggregate activities and make more transparent the cost of transactions and the level of activity-costing, so managers will need to become more aware of the actual costs of the particular activities and facilities for which they are responsible. At present, all too many choices are made on the basis of inadequate financial information and with no awareness of the actual costs incurred through commissioning any particular activity. At the most simple level, all local government staff will have been familiar with the periodic edict about 'no phone calls out of the office before 1 pm.' Whilst this minor economy represented a worthwhile effort to reduce unnecessary costs within the council, it is interesting to observe that hardly any council is in a position to attach an accurate cost to the most likely alternative form of communication – a letter. If the consequence of preventing people from telephoning, at a cost which is known but relatively insignificant, is to force them into writing, at a cost which is unknown and considerably greater, then the net result is unlikely to be an effective one. Of course, at present that may be of no consequence to an individual manager since the cost of telephone calls may be disaggregated and allocated to that unit whereas the cost of preparing letters may or may not. However, if we look to a further extension of current trends in financial management it seems likely that the arrangement that will be sought in many public service organisations is a complete disaggregation of costs to individual units and 'cost centres'. There is to date little experience of this happening in local government, and as yet it appears unlikely we can draw conclusions about how effective such a process is. Similar initiatives are being attempted within central government, and the Department of Trade and Industry operates a 'hard-charging' regime for a number of its internal services. The House of Commons committee which examined this experience came to the suitably guarded conclusion that: 'it is too early to judge whether 'hard-charging' will be successful; we will be interested in its further development' (House of Commons, 1991, p. xxxi).

Accountable managers will also need to establish appropriate levels of monitoring and control for the resources within their responsibilities. This will apply to both the monitoring and control models exercised upon them, and the forms of monitoring and control they exercise over their subordinates. In the latter case, for example, the district librarian needs to establish for the staff exactly what authority over what amount of money is given to branch librarians for the purchase of books and equipment. In relation to control and monitoring upward from the unit or cost-centre, it will be important for the manager and for the organisation that it is established quite clearly what capacity the centre has to intervene and what the implications of this intervention might be. One group of managers in a social services department described the frustration of finding that the directorate in a budgetary panic had insisted that *no* vacancies within the department would be filled, without this being agreed at a weekly directorate meeting (the stick in the wheel). Some months later, after the panic had subsided, and some three-quarters of the way through the financial year, those managers were criticised by the directorate for having underspent on their staffing budgets and urged to do something about it 'quickly'. Equally predictably, they were not able to do so and the department reached the year end underspent on staffing.

In the medium to longer term it is likely to be increasingly valuable for responsible financial managers to become aware of the different processes of investment appraisal. At present, decisions on capital expenditure are in many authorities often taken in a very different framework from those related to revenue expenditure. However, if current trends continue, and if decision-making on financial management is increasingly to be devolved to those with responsibility for particular sections or particular units, it is probable that the two streams of decision-making on revenue and capital will move closer together. Thus it will become important for the relevant manager to understand different approaches to investment appraisal and, for example, be able to assess the relative benefits of a equipment or plant choice based on high capital and low continuing revenue, or vice versa. At present, in many authorities such decisions are rarely taken by the same person or people in any common forum. If the quality of financial management within local government is to improve, and the responsibilities for that management are to be genuinely delegated from the centre to other subordinate managers within the organisations, then other changes must necessarily take place within the council.

How must the organisation change?

As with any major organisational change, to assume simply that if the relevant people knew more, then the organisation would operate more effectively without the need for organisational change, is a dangerous illusion. It is not enough for individuals to understand that there are different ways of doing things and that they are equipped to do them in different ways, but the organisation itself must provide them with the necessary support mechanisms and encouragement of new practice for there to be effective organisational change. There are a number of critical organisational aspects where local authorities must make these changes, and some councils are making major advances in doing so. Others are constrained by resource limitations – for, perhaps, a capital investment programme in new technology – or, and sadly more often, because of a reluctance at the centre to accept the implications and consequences of broader organisational change. One of the major factors will be the ability of the authority to create support-systems for managers which provide current and useful information about current budgets, levels of expenditure and commitments which may either be implicit in continuing programmes or which the decision-maker has already entered into. The most frequent observation that managers with financial responsibility make about the support they receive from within the organisation is that it is outdated, and does not provide them with financial information that is consistent with their pattern of organisation and decision-making. In such circumstances, the temptation is for the person placed in this position to create alternative information and support-systems, which may range from an inadequate accounts book bought from the local stationery store to a personal computer with a proprietary accounting system on it. While this may provide a short-term solution to immediate needs – though not always a very reliable one – it has the potential to create enormous difficulties by establishing two often inconsistent streams of information about the same resource commitments within the organisation. In the longer term it is not effective, and we would argue that it serves by default to perpetuate central systems which do not meet the management requirements of operational decision-makers within the organisation.

If the council wishes to ensure that organisational change does occur, and that appropriate decisions are delegated to accountable managers, then it will be necessary to create and support management information systems that can be interrogated by those managers at varying levels of detail. In those councils which are moving towards this arrangement but did not have the necessary information systems to support it, it is quite usual to find, in many managers' offices, a dusty-looking pile of computer print out that clearly has not been looked at since it arrived in the office. The more effective councils are now increasingly likely to have an on-line information system, which is accessible through an office PC or screen and allows a manager to roam around the detail of actual spending, commitment and projected income for the appropriate unit information within the department. Clearly, some staff will not be comfortable with that level of access at first and will probably generate a great deal of additional work and inquiries for the finance department. Within the longer term, such a process of learning and familiarisation is necessary for the organisation to ensure genuine accountability from managers in that kind of position.

A budget is a very important device for planning and for achieving control within the organisation. It should have the capacity to motivate and encourage staff to feel they have some responsibility for managing a budget, and delivering the services and activities which are expressed in monetary form through that budget. The traditional model of budget preparation is both highly centralised and often – if not actually secret – confined to a relatively limited circle of people. It does not serve as a device for motivating managers, let alone staff, as they often feel they have no say in its creation or composition. All of the forces for change which are leading local authorities to think about delegating more responsibility should equally be suggesting to them the need to open up the budgetary process, to ensure the choices are more broadly discussed, and that information about possible courses of action is more broadly shared amongst those several hundred people (in a typical medium sized council) who actually have the responsibility for delivering on that budget. All too often at present, the way in which the system of budget setting and financial planning operates effectively excludes those people from the process and therefore even serves to make some of them see their main task as *evading* the main thrust of budget decisions. That phenomenon is compounded by the lack of capacity in current financial systems to reward – not personally but in organisational terms – those parts of the organisation which either do a good job on delivering on the budget or are able to find innovative and creative ways of delivering on their service commitments under a budget. It is convenient and easy for all such decisions to be made by a relatively closed circle of people operating in the centre of the organisation; it is not effective in the longer term in creating a flexible and responsible organisation, with managers accountable for their actions and able to deliver a more responsive service.

If local authorities are increasingly to delegate responsibility to operational managers then they will necessarily have to be very clear about the limits of that delegation and the authority that they delegate along with that responsibility. A typical job description for an operational manager with financial responsibilities in local government may read as follows:

'To manage financial resources delegated to the disability team, determining and gaining acceptance for priorities allocating budgets, delegating responsibility, authorising and keeping expenditure within the budgetary allocations, in order to ensure the most cost effective use of resources' (manager – aids and adaptations, social services department).

This example is deliberately chosen because the expenditure of funds on practical measures of support for people with a disability characterises all of the classic dilemmas that the spending manager in local government faces. Assessment of need is often carried out according to poorly defined criteria; planning to commit and spend money can occur over a relatively long time-scale because of the complexity of agreeing exactly what is to be done. It is also the kind of local government service where effective reductions in expenditure – perhaps at a mid-year point of crisis – can only be achieved by reining back on demand, effectively by making the criteria for agreement to expenditure more rigorous and demanding. The operational manager may therefore have delegated authority which is then suspended or constrained by crisis at the centre of the organisation.

Many of the changes that we are seeing in public management in general, and in the management of local authorities in particular, are intended to make those organisations more responsive to the user and consumer of public services. In order to create and effectively support that degree of responsiveness, one of the other areas of change that must be considered by local government is introducing greater flexibility into decision-making. There is an understandable fear amongst members that an over emphasis on flexibility will see arbitrary decisions being made by different officials within different departments and in different areas within the authority. Implicit in such a fear is a clear assumption that officials can't be trusted. This goes beyond any perception of individual weakness or failure, and is in itself a reflection of a broader strategic failure to agree a clear purpose and strategy for the organisation. One aspect of financial management where this is at its most pronounced is in the fees and charges that local authorities collect from companies and individuals for various services provided. It is often observed that, regardless of party, many councils appear to find it exceptionally difficult to discuss charges for any services, ranging from house rents to the charge for a deckchair on the beach. As a direct consequence of this uncertainty and hesitation all too many councils have been content to rely on the ratchet affect of inflation to allow them to increase charges on an across the-board-basis, regardless of any other considerations which price-setters elsewhere might take into account. While in a public service it would be inappropriate to haggle and argue prices on the basis of market trading, there are many services provided by local authorities where an important element of management discretion would be the capacity to change prices which respond to local circumstance and peak time/quiet time demand, in pools and leisure centres, for example. If the operational manager is to respond effectively to changing circumstance then he or she requires the authority to do this, outside the framework of the traditional annual report to committee which sets charges for all facilities and activities across the authority regardless of local circumstance. Within the framework of a broad strategic direction for the organisation it should be possible to create a regime whereby councillors are able to trust this and similar decisions to managers who are nearer to the day-to-day practice of the service than they are.

Some of the changes suggested above pose a considerable challenge to the assumptions that are made about the ways in which local authorities are run. It is important not to underestimate the effort and time required to plan for such change, put it into effect, and create the climate within the organisation at all levels which will effectively support such change. Nonetheless it is necessary because there continue to be indications that the broad direction of such change is on the policy agenda for the current government (and would probably be so for any likely alternative government). Even some long-established and hallowed traditions of public financial management are now subject to challenge and review as other organisational change occurs. For example, a discussion document on 'devolved school management' published by the Scottish Office (1992) refers to the traditional practise of 'annuality' in a one-sentence paragraph. 'Subject to the normal audit requirements, and any other necessary safeguards, schemes should allow for budget surpluses and deficits to be carried forward from one financial year to the next' (p. 7). If the government is able to suggest such radical changes, in such a casual reference, then many other changes will also be in prospect as well.

Some points for discussion

1. Does your council make budget decisions through a 'star chamber' or similar body?
2. If you are a council manager, how much expenditure do you actually control?
3. Does your council think clearly about prices and charges?
4. How does the council shift resources into developing new activities from declining services?

6 Managing Competitively

The pre- and postwar period of growth and development for local government saw a major increase in the variety and volume of services provided by local authorities to the community. The period saw not simply an increase in the size and scale of local government but an increasing tendency to assume that newly developing public services should be provided by local authorities. The assumptions underlying the reform discussion of the late 1960s and early 1970s clearly envisaged a growing and continually increasing role for local authorities. The observations of the Royal Commission which reviewed local government in Scotland are typical:

> So far as local government services are concerned, we are assured on all hands that only in rare cases will they decline in importance. . . . Public opinion is resigned to – and indeed demands – more and more intervention by public authorities. . . . Services can no longer be conceived in isolation from one another, or from their place in the total pattern of the activities of society (Wheatley, 1969, para. 94).

The clear assumptions that underlay the two reorganisations of the mid-1970s were that local government would come to be responsible for an ever-wider variety of activities and services, and that those activities and services would increase in volume and scale. For this reason – and for others – the conclusions arrived at led to the recommendation of fewer and larger local authorities and a slackening of some of the controls which central government had previously placed on local government. Twenty years later, it is clear that the government has a very different view of what local government should be responsible for, how it should be shaped, and how it should organise itself to secure the delivery of necessary services and facilities to the community. The government now considers that local authorities will be more effective and more efficient if they provide fewer services directly themselves, instead procuring others to do so. It also places much emphasis on the benefits that are claimed to arise from public services being competitively tested in various ways against alternative competitive providers or alternative forms of provision.

The 'Citizen's Charter' (HM Government, 1991a, p. 4) claims that increased competition in the provision of public services is one very important way of improving the quality of those services. 'In a free market, competing firms must strive to satisfy their customers, or they will not prosper. Where choice and competition are limited, consumers cannot as easily or as effectively make their views count. In many public services, therefore, we need to increase both choice and competition where we can.'

As will be shown below, the government's commitment to competition and the view that it will provide a powerful spur to improving the quality of public services has not necessarily been a consistent and clear theme in the raft of changes that have occurred in the provision of public services. It is however a dominant trend in the government's approach to public services, and one which has come to exert a powerful influence on the organisation and delivery of local authority services. The actual volume of activities which are now formally subject to some form of competitive tendering are substantial, having increased from somewhere in the order of one hundred million pounds per annum in the late 1980s to more than two thousand million pounds per annum by early 1993 (Audit Commission, 1993). In volume terms this is significant, though in comparative terms it stills represents a small proportion of the total expenditure activity of local government in Britain. Nonetheless the impact that this has had on thinking about local government has been spectacular. Whereas in the heyday of local government it was assumed that 'the council will do it', now it is the common currency of discussion in local government to hear senior staff and members talking openly about the possibility that some other organisation or agency can carry out a function – whether a direct service or an internal activity that has previously been the responsibility of directly employed staff.

The impact of competition is not only seen in those services which are legally required to be tested in the market by competitive tender. There are many other services where the prospect of competition, or the legislative, financial, and regulatory changes that have led to an increased emphasis on individual choice and competition between providers has produced a very different approach to managing the organisation and delivering services. In the provision of housing, the shift in government strategy from sale to sitting tenants to an encouragement of mass opting-out from local authority ownership and the move to other forms of landlord has encouraged dramatic changes in the way in which local authority housing departments are run. Stoker (1991, p. 215) observes that: 'both politicians and housing officials have chosen to preserve their role as social landlords by *winning the competition*; improving their relationship with tenants and seeking to retain their support' (emphasis added). Those schools which have opted out of local authority control are clearly now in an overtly competitive position. Even those schools which have remained with the local authorities often attempt to put themselves in a position where they will be viewed as more successful and therefore more desirable than neighbouring schools. The colleges of further education, which left local authority control in April 1993, have – certainly in the urban centres – politely competed against each other for many years now. In a wide range of public services, and particularly within the various services provided by local government, there has been a major cultural shift which now leads many members and senior staff to talk in terms which would have been considered inappropriate even a few years ago. So for example, early in 1993, one social services department advertised for a general manager for what is, in effect, the direct service operation providing residential and day-care services for those in contact with the social services department. The advertisement sought to attract somebody who would be 'initially tackling the strategic development and business planning, you'll then get to grips with marketing the new organisation services, establishing close and effective relationships with both customers and commissioning agencies'. The department is seeking in the appointee for this post a 'fundamental grasp of public service delivery and its anticipated future environment – with complementary budgetary, communication, management and negotiating skills' (*Guardian*, May 1993).

To a considerable extent, then, the language of competition and the marketplace is now readily apparent in the way in which we describe and discuss public services. This chapter examines a number of the significant elements that have contributed to these circumstances arising. We look first at the background in local government and the development of formalised competitive working arrangements in recent years. The changes that have occurred in local government and the way in which organisations have responded to the requirements of competition are considered, along with the range of new skills and approaches necessarily required by managers operating in a competitive environment. The final part of the chapter will then examine some possible future outcomes for a wide range of local government services, and the implications for those who work in them.

Background

Until the early 1980s councils had a broad discretion as to the various organisational mechanisms they used to provide services either to the public or internally to the organisation. The precise mix of services provided by or through the directly employed workforce or by external suppliers was more often than not a reflection of historic circumstance, local requirement, the broad operating environment of the particular local council and – though often to quite a limited extent – the political views of the majority of members. So the rise of direct labour in local government – particularly in construction and related services – was in some authorities the subject of considerable political debate and dispute. The predecessor to the Greater London Council, the old London County Council, was in its early years riven by political argument about whether or not the council should carry through its slum clearance and rebuilding programmes using private contractors or direct labour. This argument focused both on the practical trades of construction and on the supervisory and architectural practises of the council, and was the subject of partisan difference at local elections.

In other local authorities, while Conservative members might not be as enthusiastic about directly employed construction staff as were many Labour members, this did not mean that such councils had no direct labour-force – they did. In other fields of council activity the manner in which particular services were delivered would vary substantially from place to place. Many coastal resort and holiday towns, for example, though often under Conservative control or influence, usually had an extensive array of services which were provided by directly employed staff rather than being contracted out to private providers. The underlying reason for this was that such activities were so central to the success of the town or resort it was seen as being vital that they should be retained in local authority control. Generally speaking, then, local authorities would use their discretion to establish what they thought to be the mix of service provision most appropriate to the circumstances of the particular council. Conservative councils might be generally antipathetic to directly employed labour, and Labour councils generally supportive. However, factors other than party control and ideology, such as scale and significance, were a significant element in making choices.

Whilst local political decisions influenced the actual size and importance of a directly employed construction workforce, the general pattern of service delivery for a wide variety of local government services was pretty much the same throughout the United Kingdom. The major construction projects in roads, structures and buildings were designed and managed by internally employed staff, and in the great majority of cases were let on competitive tender to major construction companies. The purchase of goods and materials was carried out through some form of public advertisement and tender – though often of a fairly rudimentary and unsophisticated nature. The bulk of local authority activities outside the construction field were generally provided and delivered by directly employed staff. Certainly the closer the service was to the centre of the organisation the more likely this would be. Legal and administrative services, financial management, planning, the strategic control of roads and highways and education services, would generally all be provided by direct employees of the council. In some of the very small councils which existed prior to the 1974 and 1975 reorganisation, legal work and clerking services were occasionally provided by a local solicitor working on a part-time or fee basis, but generally the vast bulk of local authority activities were carried out by directly employed staff.

Conservative governments did on occasion attempt to discourage the growth of direct labour, mainly in the construction industries. The Labour government of the 1960s made some tentative moves towards reviewing council practises on direct labour and construction, but until the 1970s there was no overall considered move against the councils' discretion to determine whether or not they provided particular services through directly employed staff or brought in contractors to carry out those activities. The accession of a Conservative government in 1979 marked a major watershed in the introduction of competition into the provision of local government services.

The development of competition

The Conservative government elected in 1979 was committed to economic policies dramatically different from those of its predecessors. The major programme of institutional change initiated by that government was to a great degree intended as a means of promoting that economic strategy. A number of themes of policy development were significant for the public sector generally, and for local government in particular. Some of those were related to reshaping the institutional framework – the 'supply-side' policies of the government. Others were more simply expressed in terms of reducing the proportion of gross domestic product committed to the public sector.

There were therefore three main elements of policy towards the public sector which that government introduced. They wanted to reduce expenditure, to improve efficiency in the public sector and, in particular, to limit trade-union influence in the public sector. They also saw scope for the privatisation of some activities which had been associated with the public domain for many years. The actual form that the 'privatisation' took varied considerably in different areas of the public sector, and indeed was not necessarily a consistent programme – despite later retrospective claims that it was. In local government, the main form taken by this attempt to move activities out of the public sector was the requirement that a greater proportion of local authority activities be established on a basis that tested them against potential alternative providers in the private sector.

The initial means of enforcing these changes in the public sector was through the Local Government (Planning and Land) Act of 1980, which required all local authorities to put most of their building construction, major engineering and maintenance work to some form of test through competitive tender. The Act was very detailed and specific, and it required local authorities to create particular institutional forms: Direct Labour Organisations (DLOs), with separate accounting systems and other organisational elements which were intended to create a distinct separation between the contracting arm of the authority and the client arm of the department which required the work to be done (housing, roads, etc.). Most local authorities established one or more of these direct labour organisations with a separate organisational form and structure and a separation from the department of which they had previously been a part.

When construction and maintenance works were being planned, the work had to be specified by the client department, and for most work it was necessary to advertise the availability of that work publicly and invite tenders from interested and eligible contractors. The DLO was required to submit a tender along with any other interested bidders from the private sector. Although authorities were allowed to make some judgement on the suitability of particular contractors to carry out work, by and large the expectation of the legislation was that work would be awarded to the lowest tenderer. Because these DLOs were still part of the local authority, the government insisted that it would be necessary for them to demonstrate their efficiency in winning and delivering contracts by showing a target rate of return on the total assets they employed as part of their operation. Such organisations were required to keep separate accounts and to record their achievement in meeting this rate of return. The capital employed was measured on a current cost accounting basis – another departure for local government practice – and the rate of return was calculated on the basis of the current year operating surplus as a percentage of the current value of capital employed to do all the work. If DLOs consistently fell short of the required rate of return over a number of years then the relevant government department (Environment, Welsh or Scottish Office) could require them to be shut down.

The way in which the 1980 Act was implemented in many local authorities was important in a number of respects for the way in which it set the general climate on which the whole basis of competition within local government is discussed. It required a specific formal separation of the body specifying the work and the one carrying it out. The power of departmental influence in local government has long been so significant that this separation compounded the creation of an 'us and them' feeling among many local government employees who had previously worked together in one unified operation. In one study of the impact of subsequent competitive tendering legislation the authors report a building maintenance manager for one Scottish district resenting the way in which he was viewed by colleagues in the housing department as 'just another contractor' (Kerley and Wynn, 1991). The legislation also required local authorities to define, itemise, and cost activities in a far more rigorous way than had previously been the case. This in itself began to create disciplines which subsequently had a considerable influence on the organisational form and management practices of local government. Because of the familiarity in the construction trades with the processes of specifying work, defining activities and tendering, many local authorities – though perhaps resentful of the imposition of legislation – were able to see that the process could be carried out. It could also often lead to a more successful DLO, which in some cases began to win more work than might previously have been the case under a voluntary regime for construction-related projects. Nonetheless, sufficient authorities resented and resisted the legislation for the government to continue to introduce a range of regulatory and statutory instruments during the 1980s, which increasingly restricted the capacity of local authorities to use their discretion as to which work they put out to enforced competitive tender. By the late 1980s, therefore, much of the construction-related activity of local government had fully adjusted to the expectation of operating within a competitive regime.

During the mid-1980s the government continued to develop its ideas on the introduction of competition into public services, and expressed its broad ambitions most clearly in a consultation paper *Competition in the Provision of Local Authority Services* (HM Government, 1985). This document outlined the various services which the government thought should be exposed to more competition, and there were two initial attempts in the late 1980s to introduce legislation to this effect. Eventually the government secured the passing of the Local Government Act 1988, which was intended to ensure that 'local and other public authorities undertake certain activities only if they can do so competitively' (Section 1). The government had clearly learned from the experience of earlier competitive tendering legislation, because in effect the 1988 Act is a piece of enabling legislation which allows further activities to be brought within the requirements of the Act through a relatively simple parliamentary procedure – as occurred with leisure management in late 1989.

The 1988 Act obliged local authorities, within a tight time-scale, to invite tenders for 'defined activities', and debarred them from providing that service through a directly employed workforce unless that in-house operation has been tested through open competition against alternative possible providers. A number of activities were defined in the initial legislation: vehicle maintenance, ground maintenance, building cleaning, street cleaning, refuse collection, school and welfare catering and other forms of catering (civic hospitality, canteens, etc.). The requirement of the legislation is that if an authority wishes to continue to have such work done by an in-house operation it needs to create a distinct organisation capable of bidding for work specified and supervised by a separate unit of the local authority. With some exceptions, most local authorities responded to this by creating what they generally called Direct Service Organisations, which were organised to act as a contractor delivering to an agreed price the works required by a 'client' section of the council. There were some limitations on the requirement to put work out to tender, but these were only significant for very small councils with a limited volume of expenditure on such activities.

Authorities were required to test work on a tendered basis even when there were no other potential bidders from the private sector seeking to carry out that work. In the event that this was the case and that the contract was won by the in-house operation, the terms of the tender had to still be met or the relevant secretaries of State had powers to intervene against the local authority. The legislation also required local authorities not to place limitations which were seen as being 'uncommercial' on contractors, although they were required to observe certain parts of the Race Relations Act, 1976. This debarred councils from requiring contractors to meet minimum standards in areas such as staff training and equal opportunities.

In effect, the legislation of the 1988 Act, as with the 1980 Act, required councils to treat certain parts of their operations as being much on a par with the private contractors who worked in the same field. No favours were to be given, no special privileges were to be enjoyed, and if unsuccessful or potential commercial contractors felt that this was occurring then they had the opportunity to complain about it to the government – an opportunity which some of them took up. The two pieces of legislation and the related regulations created a climate in which local authorities were obliged to think 'competitively', and under which they suffer sanctions from the government if they operate on a 'anti-competitive' basis.

After successive rounds of competitive tendering under the 1980 Act a sizable – though still comparatively small – proportion of local authority expenditure is now committed to delivering services and functions on a tendered basis, whether the tender was won by an external contractor or by internal contracting organisations. The actual volume in cash terms – some £2.5 thousand million in early 1993 – is a great deal of money, although not compared to the totality of local authority budgets. The process has, however, created a dramatic and long-term impact in all local authorities. In a report on the impact of competitive tendering the Audit Commission accurately titled one chapter 'The world has changed' (Audit Commission, 1993).

The world has changed not simply for those DLOs and DSOs which are now required to submit tenders on a competitive basis for the work which they might previously have assumed to be theirs as a right. The world has also changed for other parts of the organisations; everyday discussion in many parts of local government is now conducted in familiar terms about a division between 'client' and 'contractor'. The impact has also been felt in central departments of the typical local authority (legal, finance and personnel), which have traditionally been used to exerting detailed and often highly prescriptive control over service departments. The requirement to operate on a competitive basis has forced those central departments to come to a relationship with service departments that recognises that they are providing a service which must be specified and costed in one way or another. The most popular way of doing this has been for interdepartmental arrangements to be agreed on the basis of a service-level agreement which is frequently represented through a formal document, on occasion signed and dated by the senior staff concerned, such as the director of finance and the director of housing. Such agreements have no formal legal standing, as the council as a whole is a unitary legal entity, but they do represent a very powerful discipline which requires central departments to demonstrate that they are providing an effective service, of the kind that the client department wants, and at a cost (and price) which is acceptable to the client department. Most importantly these factors of costs and service are capable of being assessed in advance or at the time of operation rather than on a post hoc basis.

The evidence available of broader change in local government as a response to the competition requirements of the 1980 and – in particular – the 1988 Act suggested at the time that the impact of competition was working itself through virtually all of the different parts and departments of local authorities. There might have been a good case for the government leaving well alone and allowing the effects of competition to secure change in all parts of local government. However, perhaps for broader political reasons, the government had decided by 1991 that it wished to extend compulsory introduction of various forms of competition to a number of different public services. In late 1991 the government published over the signature of the Chancellor of the Exchequer a White Paper whose front cover captured in different ways the interlinked strands of the governments strategic drive on public services. The document was entitled *Competing for Quality* with the subtitle *Buying Better Public Services*, and badged with the logo of the Citizen's Charter 'Raising the standard'. In his foreword the Chancellor outlined the government's ambition:

> The Citizen's Charter sets out the Governments wish to improve public services. We aim to make public services respond better to the wishes of the users – above all by expanding choice and competition.
>
> This White Paper, which sets out how we propose to expand competition in the public sector, is a key part of the Citizen's Charter programme. It emphasises the role of public sector managers in buying services on behalf of citizens. Services may be bought either from the private sector or within the public sector: we have no dogmatic preference for either one over the other. We believe that the best private sector managers and the best public services can match anything achieved in the public sector. And we believe that public sector managers and staff will welcome the opportunity to compare the services that they provide in fair and open competition with the best of the private sector (p. ii).

In those opening two paragraphs, the entire government rationale and programme for introducing competition into public services is clearly underlined.

A linked consultation paper *Competing for Quality – Competition in the Provision of Local Services* (HM Government, 1991c) outlined government plans to extend competition in a number of local authorities' services. In what are described as the manual services, it proposed introducing competition into police support services, the maintenance of fire vehicles, and school transport. Certain services provided directly to the public, including the management of libraries and arts facilities, along with parking, were also to be considered for forms of competition. Among internal services, all of the professional property services (architecture, engineering and property management) were proposed for competitive testing. At the very heart of the local authority, the corporate services, of administration, legal services, finance, personnel and computing were also to be subject to some form of market test. In the case of these central corporate services there were varying proportions of these activities which it was suggested should be exposed to some form of competition. The consultation paper also proposed a tightening-up of the regulations which surrounded the management of competition, on the basis of government claims that 'too many authorities have bent over backwards to ensure that contracts have been awarded to their own work forces, for example in the face of lower bids from private contractors' (p. 2). The consultation proved particularly controversial in local government circles. There were several reasons for this: most obviously, such proposals seem to go to the very heart of activities which local government had tradition-ally viewed as being self-evidently best provided by directly employed staff immediately accountable to the council and under direct council control. More broadly based opposition to the government proposals was encouraged by leaked information which suggested that even government advisors had considerable doubts about whether the proposals would be capable of effective implementation. Perhaps most persuasive of the objections was the recognition that such proposed changes coincided directly with government plans for reorganisation of local government, and would consume the energies and effort of all those people at the centre of the local authority most concerned with effecting any reorganisation plans. After consideration of this, the government deferred plans for an extension of competitive tendering until after reorganisation has been completed.

The impact of competition has not only been felt in those services and activities required to introduce compulsory competitive tendering. The opening part of this chapter suggested that the significance of the major change in local government thinking was at a wider level in the organisation. In effect, the change that has occurred in local government has been a shift in the culture and values of the organisation. Although there has been, and continues to be, much discussion about what we mean by the 'culture' of organisations, there does seem to be some substance to the argument that different organisations do things in different ways and absorb into their practice a complex and sometimes confused mixture of procedures, values and assumptions, all of which can reasonably be described as the culture of the organisation. Local authorities now operate in a competitive environment, and members, managers, and the staff who work within the organisation increasingly see their position as one of competition, sometimes against external alternative providers and sometimes against colleagues within the same institutional framework. The impact of this shift can be seen in those services designated as subject to competitive tendering, and services which have been the subject of other forms of legislative change.

This is very clearly part of the government's broader intention to inject competition into the provision of public services. In education, the major changes made in England and Wales in the late 1980s were heralded by the then Secretary of State Kenneth Baker as a means to: 'Galvanise parental involvement in schools. Parents will have more choice. They will have greater variety of schools to choose from. We will create new types of schools . . . introduce competition into the public provision of education. This competition will introduce a new dynamic into our schools system which will stimulate better standards all around' (quoted in Ranson, 1990, p. 23).

In social work, one of the major themes of the new legislation for 'community care' has been the linking of choice and competition. Amongst the key objectives outlined in the White Paper *Caring for People* (HM Government, 1989, p. 5) were listed: 'to promote the development of a flourishing interdependent sector alongside good quality public services. . . . Packages of care should then be designed in line with individual needs and preferences.' In the foreword to the document the various secretaries of state involved claimed 'our aim is to promote choice as well as independence'.

The impact of competition – changes in the organisation

The changes that have seen a wide range of local government services now operating within a competitive environment have required modifications in the form of the organisations, discussed in this section, and also the development of new skills on the part of those responsible for managing such services. For those services which have been defined as being subject to compulsory tendering, councils have had to make clearly prescribed changes in the way in which they are organised. The organisational forms used have varied a little, but essentially councils have been obliged to define clearly those parts of the organisation which will carry out contracting responsibilities. They have also been required, as described above, to create separate accounting arrangements for services delivered in this way.

The legal requirement to create these organisational forms obliged councils to carry out often fundamental reviews of their organisation. In many cases the services under review had rarely been examined in any detail by the authority over many years. Indeed, one of the most significant aspects of the 1988 changes were that they caused many councils to look hard at the management of services which, to a great extent, had often previously not had significant management input. Services such as catering and cleaning, for example, had not previously carried much weight within the organisation and were often simply assumed to be the responsibility of relatively junior officials, to be provided simply as a matter of course. The competitive shift has lead to an increased tendency in local authorities to think more clearly in terms of a separation between client and contractor. It has had the effect of separating financing from the provision of services, which has required the council to be clear about the organisation of the contracting function and to have determined the shape of that part of the organisation which is to carry out the tasks. It has also had to clarify the role of the client function within the authority and to establish a clear division of duties and responsibilities in a way that has often proved difficult for all of those involved.

The traditional assumption of local authority management and decision-making has been that a committee decision, the initiative of an officer, or even a request from an individual member, translates more or less directly into action by the organisation on the ground – given the availability of resources and the capacity to vary actions within those resource-constraints. The regulated shift to a different regime for compulsorily tendered services and the other changes that have affected a variety of other local authority services require a far more arms-length approach on the part of the client side of the organisation. Thus the client side has had to learn new skills and adapt to new forms of organisational decision-making.

The council has had organisationally to think far more in terms of broad policy definition, which is then translated into a specification of services to be delivered – potentially by an external contractor who is not part of the council. In order to manage this process effectively it has become necessary for the council to work in terms of letting and managing a contract, and in some areas of activity this has often been a contract which is finely detailed and extensive in its nature. Because of changing expectations, and because contracts specifications may be weak, the organisation then has to equip itself not simply to monitor the contract as prescribed, but also to review the performance of the contractor and the service in order to think longer term about how that contracted arrangement might be delivered in a different and more effective way. The council has therefore to review performance effectively, and not simply monitor a particular contract. All of these factors contribute to a need for a very different type of organisation to that which the local councils have traditionally had. The Audit Commission has taken a particularly strong view on what organisational arrangements councils should adopt, and recommends separation between members responsible for the client function – traditional manner – and members sitting on a DSO 'board'. At an official level it suggests there should be a clear distinction between a client department – again in traditional fashion – and a contract supervision unit and either a DSO for particular services or an umbrella DSO to manage a variety of services.

The arrangements that most councils have arrived at have generally had the effect of doing what the government's reform programme for local government management partly intended to achieve – the greater separation of management from politics. That process in turn has lead to a requirement for those officials who manage in the new competitive environment to think about the necessary array of skills that they must acquire and develop.

The new skills of management in a competitive climate

Despite resistance to the idea of imposed tendering, local authorities generally felt themselves reasonably well equipped to cope with the competitive requirements of the 1980 legislation. They were less confident in dealing with the services that were made subject to competitive tender in the 1988 legislation. Both in form of organisation and in staffing available, many local authorities were at first uncomfortable with and concerned about the prospect of facing competition. The different stages of anticipation and expectation through which local authorities have passed have been described elsewhere as: fear and loathing, confident comparison, and wary acceptance (Kerley and Wynn, 1991). The reaction of authorities in the first phase led them in many cases to doubt whether they had the management capacity within the organisation to cope with the demands of competition. Their reaction in this case was often to seek to recruit from outside local government those whom they assumed would have the appropriate mix of necessary management skills – usually, though not always, gained in the private sector.

In many cases, it does seem that the fear of lack of internal management capacity was unfounded. Many local authority staff have adjusted effectively and well to the demands of operating in a competitive environment. In doing so they have had to acquire and develop many new skills, as managers operating within a very different regime from that traditionally associated with local government services. The broader challenge of competition now faced by many authorities in many services will make it necessary for these new skills to be understood by other managers as they face the challenge of competition. These new management skills and processes have not generally been part of the repertoire of managers in the public services but have had to become so, though in a way that is effectively adapted to the particular context of a public service regime. Merely mimicking the practices that may be appropriate in a confectionery firm has not worked, nor is it consistent with the values of public service. There are however certain key areas of business management practice which the new generation of public managers will have to understand and adapt to their particular circumstances.

Business planning

There are numerous proprietary approaches to business planning, several of which are discussed in any of the basic textbooks. Perhaps the most important element of business planning that a local government manager can usefully understand is that the process is quite simply one intended to help the organisation adjust to a changing external environment. This is of course vitally important for an organisation which trades in a market. For local government agencies such an adjustment has often not been a major concern. There are numerous local authorities which have seen a long-term secular decline in the demand for (say) school places, yet have avoided over many years employing the appropriate analyses and planning processes that would have helped them to address that decline. As more and more local government agencies and institutions find themselves operating in a competitive environment they will necessarily have to think about the strengths and weaknesses, the opportunities and threats, which are aspects of one the most popular and widespread business planning approaches.

Marketing

Marketing is about establishing the right relationship between the provider of a service or facility and the users, consumers, purchasers, and beneficiaries or that service or facility. Local government has often been slow to understand the requirements of a base of changing users and consumers. In discussing housing, members will often refer to 'proper family housing' with limited recognition of the degree to which a pattern of demand for local authority housing has changed dramatically in the past twenty to twenty-five years and the extent to which a two adult, 2–4 children family is now a distinct minority in our society.

Members, and managers, are now beginning to apply far more sophisticated analysis to thinking about exactly who uses local authority services. Consideration must be given not merely to numbers – though that in itself may be important – but also to the composition of users and the different demands that they may have of the services they enjoy. A lot of very interesting work is being done in many different local authority departments, particularly in those like recreation and housing. It will however have to become the norm for managers in all other departments to think far more clearly about their understanding of the users – and the non-users – of the services that they provide. Marketing will have to be seen as more than simply 'promotion', and local authority managers will have to think in terms which are routinely applied in settings where the consumer has a wide choice of service or product and provider.

Handling management information

Whether competing to deliver an agreed contract or working in a competitive relationship with other potential providers, the local government manager will have to be comfortable handling management information, both financial and of a broader nature. The established forms of appropriation budgeting have placed a great emphasis on the preparatory work of an annual budget-round – often driven from the centre. The occasional mid-year examination of figures will then see its culmination in a frantic rush toward the end of the financial year to spend the balance of that appropriation. It will increasingly become necessary for managers to have a continuous grasp on the trend and detail of the information necessary to deduct the level of demand for the service they are providing, the balance or provision of that service, and the composition of the workforce delivering that service, along with earnings and related information. In many cases they will also need to learn how important it is to be alert to cashflow and income levels.

This will, in many councils, require a complete recasting of the manner in which such management information is provided to accountable staff within the organisation. Hitherto often confined to a limited circle of staff and members at the centre, it will become necessary to make that informed circle far wider. This will require the introduction of new systems and it will also require support and training for those staff who are going to be asked to operate those systems, understand the information generated, and then act upon it.

Work and staff planning

A distinctive feature of the public services has always been the predictability of a particular type of workload for the organisation. Rubbish is always there to be collected, houses to be maintained and decorated, children and young people to be educated. The public services have not hitherto been reliant on the consumer's choice whether or not to purchase a service or a product from the organisation. Whether that choice is made through informed decision or mere whim, private companies have always been conscious of the capacity of the individual to exercise that choice and have needed to plan and organise themselves accordingly – or fail if they did not. Public managers will now increasingly find that in a competitive environment they will need to organise their activities in order to get the right balance between the demand from the consumer or user and the capacity of the organisation to provide for that demand. They may, to a degree, be aided in their planning by a contract that may extend over a number of years, but they will nonetheless need to be far more conscious of getting the right balance between demand and supply.

This will also require these managers to be far more conscious of the way in which they balance their capacity to supply with their staffing level. It is now quite common to find that in some local authorities activities such as grounds maintenance and gardening staff are on some form of annualised hours contract. In effect, this means that they work shorter hours during the winter and longer hours during the summer, giving the organisation more flexibility and a greater ability to respond to short-term requirements without the costs of overtime, premium payments, and extra temporary staff. The professional and personal services managers will also have to think in similar terms about the way in which they balance out staffing resources. In education, particularly in England and Wales, this process has occurred through default. The cash formulae developed in some areas to allow for the local management of schools have encouraged school managers to think of hiring cheaper less experienced staff as a replacement for more experienced and higher salaried staff. This seems a crude and probably shortsighted way of making decisions which may have undesirable long-term consequences. Nonetheless, in general terms, it will become necessary for service managers to think about the balance of staffing resources they have. It will probably lead them to the view that the typical and traditional pattern of staffing in local authority professional services is not suited to their new requirements. Generally speaking, many local authority professional services have had a very high proportion of professionally qualified staff with inadequate support staff to back them up. As a consequence of this, unit costs are high and – often more important – professional staff find themselves required to carry out routine activities for which there are no backup staff available, and denied the opportunity to carry out a more challenging range of demanding professional tasks. For both reasons, it will become increasingly probable that local authority managers in this position will be required to actively review the composition of their staff complement.

Management of quality

The concern for ensuring the quality of effective management is discussed from the point of view of the consumer in a later chapter; from the point of view of the service manager and provider it will become a central feature of the competitive process. The necessary concomitant of competition is choice on the part of the person who uses or consumes the service. The decision of the person or organisation receiving that service will be governed by many factors including price, convenience, familiarity, and – increasingly – quality. The manager of the providing unit will necessarily have to think of providing a quality service or facility. It will no longer be possible either to think or to say 'they'll have to take it because they don't have any choice'

Conclusion

Twenty or thirty years ago the assumptions that governed local government policy-making and management practice were essentially that 'the council does it'. Now there is hardly any corner of local government activity in which it might not be possible to imagine the presence of an alternative competitive provider, or at least such a provider being used as a device for testing the competitive quality of the service. That change will require managers to think and act in different ways. They will have to do so not simply because many of them now work in a competitive environment but because those who work in public organisations are increasingly being required to demonstrate the effective performance of those organisations.

Some points for discussion

1. Is competition between providers likely to provide a better service? If so, why? If not, why?
2. Can you see any local consequences of the competitive tendering of local authority services?
3. Are local authority managers equipped to manage competitively?
4. How can 'productivity' in council services be improved?

7 Managing Performance

In recent years there has been an increased emphasis on the performance of local government. The Audit Commission for England and Wales overstated the position when in one publication it claimed that 'performance review has always been an essential element in the management of a local authority' (1989b, p. 1). Actually, an examination of practice in many local authorities would suggest that an effective focus on performance is only now becoming part of normal management practice, and to some extent only because of legislation.

Nonetheless, the general direction of public policy is clear. Local authorities have in recent years increasingly been expected to find ways to measure their performance and to demonstrate that they are able to achieve significant improvements in performance by the more effective use of the resources available to them. This is not necessarily an easy process, particularly in local government. In the words of the Audit Commission again:

> It is often hard to measure performance in the public service, especially in terms of quality and effectiveness. However, it is wrong to overstate the difficulties. The important thing is to be clear about what each service is intended to achieve, and what distinguishes a good service from a poor one. Quality and effectiveness can be monitored in various ways, including feedback from users, and more (and better) inspection (1986, p. 4).

Councils, along with other public bodies, can find it difficult to measure and review their performance. This difficulty is often compounded by a wistful assumption that it is all much easier in the trading sector. It is somehow assumed that the publication of turnover, profit figures and earnings per share is a simple and failsafe indication of how well an organisation is doing – the famous 'bottom line'. It is interesting to note that, for example, Thames Water ceased to publish performance indicators of service-level achievement in the year that it became a PLC. Actually, measuring effective performance in large and complex organisations is very difficult. This is not a novel observation, as Drucker pointed out some twenty-five years ago: no one single yardstick is 'the' measure of performance, prospects and results of a business; '. . . success, like failure, in business enterprise is *multi-dimensional*' (Drucker, 1968, p. 85). The point he makes, of course, does not vitiate the requirement to seek ways of assessing effective performance but emphasises just how difficult it can be, even in a profit-seeking organisation.

The response to that difficulty can take a number of forms. The first is when the service professional argues that 'assessing the quality of that particular service is just too difficult and we might as well not bother, but simply take it on trust that dedicated professionals are doing this'. An alternative response is to seek even more elaborate and all-embracing ways of assessing performance. This is in some senses the route that recent governments have taken, constructing an ever more complex performance framework for public service organisations to work within. A third alternative is to recognise that there is an important political and managerial concern for the effectiveness of public services, and that there is also a perfectly legitimate and reasonable public interest in the assessment of effective performance. Because of the diversity of the interests that have a concern with performance, the appropriate response for local authorities may be to examine and develop a wide diversity of approaches to assessing performance. Rogers (1990) is very positive about the variety of different approaches that he observes in different councils: 'The mechanisms being used are immensely variable – consumer surveys, customer contracts, more realistic planning mechanisms, devolved management, and more rigorous and sensitive performance appraisals and review procedure are but a few examples. They all signify that a continuing analysis of how a local authority can improve its performance is underway' (p. 9).

There is within many councils a lot of active experimentation and discussion about the most effective ways of managing performance in local government. This chapter examines the background to this current experience, some earlier trends in local government and some more recent developments which have forced the assessment of performance more directly onto the policy agenda for many local authorities. Because of the recently introduced requirement for local authorities to publish comparative performance indicators we will examine the practice and experience of these, and consider the lessons that can be gained from other public services. The chapter will conclude by examining the implications of this emphasis on performance management for managers at a local level.

The background

It is not unreasonable to suggest that a concern for the effective management of performance simply reflects and echoes one of the themes that has underpinned conventional management theorising for much of this century – in effect, the proposition that the management process is about setting objectives and then seeking to assess progress toward those objectives. It represents in a specific form a very clear example of the 'rational planning' approach to management. Additionally, the way in which some of the leading proponents of effective performance management – for example the Audit Commission – present their ideas is very clearly based on a simple control loop system of management.

The process as presented by many advocates, and as practised in many local authorities, is heavily reliant upon assumptions of business practice and business planning. The London Borough of Ealing (1991) sees performance review and performance management as an integrated part of the business planning process. 'Performance indicators will be an integral part of the business planning process . . . the council is currently introducing a Performance Management System for chief officers. It is important – and already council policy – that this system be linked to the business planning process.' The committee report from which this quotation is drawn includes a draft business plan framework in diagrammatic form, and a modified version of this is shown in Figure 7.1. This approach to managing performance has developed from a common background in the various different approaches and forms of analysis applied to strategic business planning which have been transferred into the public services. The post-World War II wave of such ideas was led by 'management by objectives' (MBO), a process first clearly articulated by Drucker in the early 1950s in *The Practice of Management*. The ideas expressed there came to have a

FIGURE 7.1   Modified business planning framework

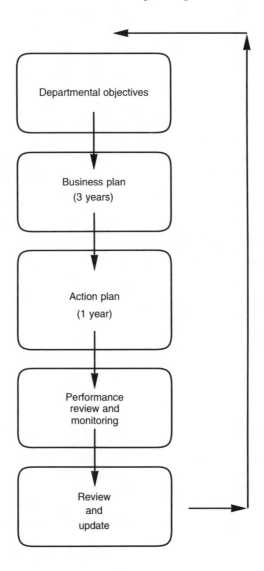

Source: London Borough of Ealing (1991).

significant influence on the way in which managers in private and public organisations came to see management within those organisations. The theme of MBO originated in America, and was translated across into both British industry and British public services. During the 1960s and the 1970s, such ideas surfaced in different forms in the public services as PPBS (Planning, Programming and Budgeting Systems) and PAR (Programme Analysis and Review). Such approaches to large-scale planning and their occasional attempted utilisation in the public services, fitted in well with the enthusiasm of the 1960s and early 1970s for more rational and scientific approaches to decision-making. In some ways it might be seen as a curious attempt to almost depoliticise the decision-making process – and in many local authorities it was viewed with considerable suspicion by members *precisely* because of that.

The very pronounced and complex linkage between attempts to improve performance, the aspiration in some areas of public service to establish a rational planning process, and the assumption that 'business methods' would be more effective than traditional public administration approaches, can be seen in many of the early documents produced by the Audit Commission for England and Wales after its establishment in 1983. The first director, Sir John Banham, had gained earlier experience with the McKinsey consultancy, and directly imported the McKinsey '7S' model of good organisational practice into the thinking of the Audit Commission. One early publication (Audit Commission, 1986, p. 83) claims:

> economy, efficiency and effectiveness do not just happen. In almost every situation changes – often uncomfortable changes, involving people doing things differently – will be involved. Those organisations in the public and private sectors which have been successful in securing beneficial changes have created an environment that thrives on challenge and change, by managing the following elements (vision, strategy, structure, systems, staffing and skills, style) in such a way as to reinforce each other.

The combination of ideas about developing more effective performance, the supposed virtues of business approaches, and the rational approach to planning influenced the climate of ideas from the 1960s onwards in ways which had a direct impact on the organisation of public services. That was seen particularly in central government with the work of the Fulton Committee (1968) but such trends also influenced local government.

Performance trends in local government

The climate of management reform in the public sector generally also had a significant influence on local government in the late 1960s and early 1970s. The Maud Committee on the management of local government (1967) articulated the then current ideas of developing more effective management processes in local government. The evidence taken and the views expressed to the committee indicated a widespread concern – particularly among the larger authorities of various political colours – that policy and decision-making were often inefficient, slow and ineffective. The recommendations made and the discussion that surrounded the report, though not leading directly to legislative change, led many of the larger authorities to make significant changes to internal decision-making. Such changes were given a boost in some of the larger English county boroughs (such as Liverpool and Coventry) through the commissioning of internal review reports from some of the major consultancy practices. This again suggests a linkage between the business-derived strategic planning processes promoted and circulated by the big consultancies such as PA and McKinsey and the impetus for change in local government.

The consequence of the structural reorganisations of the early 1970s was a recognition among government ministers and relevant local authority members and senior staff that a reshaped local government would require a different approach to management within the organisation. As the legislation to reorganise local government was completing its passage through parliament, the government sponsored and established two committees to consider council management systems and processes in the local authorities in England (Bains, 1972) and in Scotland (Paterson, 1973). Both of these committees were heavily influenced by new ideas about corporate management and rational planning in local government – indeed, it has been suggested that each reflected a majority membership almost predisposed to come up with such proposals for change. In the event the committees clearly worked hard, took evidence and advice from existing local authority associations, professional associations, and many interested observers and participants in local government. Whilst there were some significant differences in the two reports, both came to broadly the same conclusions. The emphasis in each report was essentially to stress a requirement for more cohesive and 'corporate' management in the new local authorities.

The influence on local government at the period of reorganisation through the discussion initiated by and on the recommendations arising from the Bains and Paterson reports cannot be under-estimated in its impact on the way in which the new local authorities were run. In England and Wales the secretary of state recommended that all newly elected members should be given a copy of the Bains report by their councils; and in Scotland the secretary of state in his forward to the Paterson report stated: 'I commend the report to all present councillors, particularly to those who will be members of the statutory advisory committees, and to prospective candidates at the 1974 elections. The report will, I hope, be the first paper to be put before those who are elected to the regional, islands and district councils' (Paterson, 1973, p. vii).

In summary, both reports recommended changes to both the form of local government internal management and the processes employed in developing policy and arriving at management decisions. Unfortunately, in some ways, the emphasis of both reports – an emphasis exaggerated by the inclusion of diagrams to show suggested committee structures – rather emphasised the structure over the process. It would appear that in many cases councillors, newly elected and often unfamiliar with each other and perhaps still bearing rivalries between forcibly amalgamated authorities, grasped at the first set of reasonably sound proposals available to them for the management of their new councils. Many councils appear to have simply adopted the Paterson/Bains proposals as a piece; and it is clear from studies carried out shortly after reorganisation that in many cases the proposals were taken on 'lock, stock and barrel'. More than 90 percent of all authorities throughout the United Kingdom created policy committees, established management teams, and gave their chief executive a job description either entirely based on that recommended by Bains or broadly so. It was however in the area of performance review – a very significant element of the management *process* though not necessarily of the *structure* – that there was the weakest and least lasting response to the Bains/Paterson proposals.

The main feature of the proposals put forward by Bains (where the ideas were developed more fully) and Paterson was that a review process should be built into management and decision-making systems within the council. At member level it was suggested a performance review subcommittee should be created, probably as one of the standing committees on the policy and resources committee of each council. Little consideration was given to the actual staffing of the review process, though by implication it appears that it was seen as being one of the responsibilities of the chief executive and staffed accordingly. One of the weakest elements was the Bains view on how members should be involved in the review process. Indeed, it seems clear that this was a significant and contributory factor to the weakness and relative lack of success of the review process in many councils. The report emphasised that service committees should have responsibility for establishing the policies and performance objectives, and monitoring their implementation. The report did however suggest the review subcommittee as a 'watchdog body'. A comparison was made with the Public Accounts Committee in the House of Commons, though in curious contrast to that body it was not proposed that it should have a membership of comparable seniority and weight. It was suggested that the convenor of the review committee should be a member of the parent committee (that is, policy and resources); members should be drawn from service committees with the knowledge and experience of the areas under review. The Bains committee even claimed that 'service upon such a body would provide an excellent opportunity for the development and involvement of some of the younger members' (Bains, 1972, p. 26).

In effect, although it was argued that performance review was a significant element in the management process, responsibility for it was to be given to people within the organisation with little weight or substance at either member or officer level. Very few councils appear to have created effective arrangements that placed the responsibility for the review of policy and performance on service committees. It therefore became the responsibility of people who – at member and staff level – were both external to the service committee and department and far weaker. It is relatively easy to imagine a committee chair of twenty years' standing sitting alongside his director of comparable experience and seniority and reacting in a not particularly cooperative fashion to the suggestion of some bright young thing from the chief executive's department and a couple of 'back-bench' councillors asking them to demonstrate how well they were carrying out a particular function. The consequences of this arrangement were relatively predictable. Faced with indifference and occasionally hostility from mainline service departments, the review process was in many authorities often limited to relatively small-scale and circumscribed tasks which attracted the attention of the organisation because they enabled immediate system-rationalisation to be made and cost-savings to be achieved. Thus, for example, where half a dozen councils had been brought together it was possible for a review body to examine purchasing, transport systems and energy saving, and produce recommendations which would be seen as generally beneficial and would demonstrate significant cash savings on a recurrent basis. Thus it was the minutiae of management practice rather than major programmes and strategic issue that were being explored. The other consequence of the failure to embed the review of performance firmly into the new councils was that after a relatively short period of time many councils abandoned any other than formal arrangements for performance review to be supported at committee level, and it was in practice relegated to a second-order function on the basis of the chief officer's discretion.

The regional councils in Scotland were obliged by the secretary of state to produce 'regional reports' as a vehicle for strategic management within the authority. The report from Strathclyde Regional Council (Strathclyde, 1976) indicates the intention to build a review process into the working of the new council. 'Further to previous discussions about the monitoring of performance the committee recommends the setting up of monitoring procedures at elected member and officer level additional to those indicated . . . above and others already operated by the regional council and request the chief executive to submit an early report on the matter' (p. 46). This same document gives one very clear indication of the reasons why the period of the mid to late 1970s did not provide a particularly fruitful climate for the development of effective performance review within local government. The passage cited above was included in a chapter headed 'Financial and Corporate'. A large part of that chapter emphasised the continuing budget constraints on the recently established council and that 'the financial situation would make it difficult to retain present levels of service far less to permit any dramatic improvement in services in 1976/1977' (p. 53). The generalised support for attempts to review performance in local government was not robust enough in that initial period of post-IMF austerity to withstand the pressures of short-term budget constraint and the expedient squeezing and cutting of services. In many local authorities, the financial constraints of the mid to late 1970s were tackled in a way which did not encourage systematic evaluation of effective performance but emphasised the short-term benefit of cutting budgets where it was convenient to do so.

There were other factors that could account for the relatively shortlived experience of performance review in many authorities in the 1970s. The relative success in examining detailed house keeping and economy/efficiency measures perhaps reflects a long established tradition and practice in local government – commented on critically by the Bains report. This is the – sometimes still apparent – practice of seeing the major concentration of any service review as being focused on detailed control of input into services rather than any assessment of the output or outcomes of council services. This is seen in financial management where the perspective is that of proprietary audit and the traditional comptroller. In personnel matters there is still considerable emphasis on the 'establishment' approach to controlling numbers and the balance of staff within the organisation. In matters of organisation and management practice the traditions of work study, and organisation and methods approaches are still very strong . The Bains report cites critically a response they received from one local authority in evidence: 'Management services – i.e. O and M [Organisation and Methods] and work study', and they give this as an indication of the relative lack of sophistication in the management process they observed among many pre-reorganisation local authorities. The consequence of this was not so much a collapse of many authorities' efforts to assess performance, but more that the promise suggested by the Bains and Paterson reports did not seem to have been fulfilled.

Some recent developments

In recent years, there has still been a concentration on limiting expenditure, and in the case of many authorities this is imposed through central government controls. Nonetheless, within central government and within local government this has moved on from a simple concentration on economy and efficiency to more broad thoughts about the effective performance of the organisation and of the services it delivers to the public. This change in local government mirrored changes that were occurring in central government. In 1982 the government launched the Financial Management Initiative, as part of a renewed drive to improve management in the civil service. The White Paper (*Efficiency and Effectiveness in the Civil Service*), which described the FMI, indicated some now very familiar key principles of reformed public management:

> To promote in each department an organisation and a system in which managers at all levels have:
>
> (a) a clear view of their objectives, and means to assess and, where ever possible, measure outputs and performance in relation to those objectives;
> (b) well defined responsibility for making the best use of their resources, including a critical scrutiny of output and value for money;
> (c) the information (particularly about costs), the training and the access to expert advise that they need to exercise their responsibilities effectively (HM Government, 1982).

It is not simply a misplaced concentration on semantics to notice that the emphasis on efficiency and *effectiveness* contrasts with the introduction, shortly after the Conservative election in 1979, of Sir Derek Rayner to be a prime ministerial adviser on promoting efficiency and eliminating *waste*: This is an explicit development in government thinking and a shift in the focus on developing the effectiveness of public services. So through the 1980s and into the 1990s there was a very noticeable sense in which, despite the continuing concentration on reducing and constraining expenditure, the government had moved in its thinking away from a simple concentration of eliminating waste and economy toward a greater sense of attempting to assess the effectiveness of public services and to begin to talk about the quality of those public services. The Citizen's Charter emphasised four main themes: quality, choice, standards and value – and these were seen by the government as being interrelated. That interrelationship is a theme which has been persistently pressed by government representatives. The secretary of state responsible for public services and the Citizen's Charter was interviewed on the radio early in 1993 about the Citizen's Charter and British Rail:

> Well, of course they need investment and they get investment but it would be a very strange thing if the government and the public services were the only great corporation or supplier of goods to people in the world that didn't have a quality control department; that didn't have a constant campaign to try to raise quality. No other retail organisation, if I can make that analogy, would survive long unless they relentlessly tried to use modern ways of management and modern methods of organisation to listen to the customers and to raise standards (William Waldegrave, *Today Programme*, Radio 4, 14 April 1993).

In that short extract Waldegrave manages to pull together a number of the significant words and phrases which are seen to characterise the more effective management of public services. The period under review has seen a shift in political thinking which has led to representatives of all the major parties placing great emphasis on the effective delivery of public services. That change in attitude is illustrated by the comments made by a Labour member of the education committee in Strathclyde Region, quoted in a report on the organisation of the education department: 'There is a urgent need for the development of some simple, direct methods and procedures for monitoring what we do which will tell us if the thing we want to happen really does happen . . . we need to do this, we need to monitor what we do now. We should not pass any policy paper unless it says clearly how we intend to monitor what happens' (Inlogov, 1989).

That view from an overwhelmingly Labour council was echoed in public comment by a former member of that council who subsequently became a member of parliament and an opposition spokesman on education in Scotland. In attempting to define the Labour Party position on assessing the performance of schools, he argued: 'What we are proposing is appraising every school to see how it measures the standards we will be setting. They will be much more performance-orientated, with decent management targets' (Tony Worthington MP reported in *The Scotsman*, 1990).

In summarising the key themes that emerge from examining these recent trends in local government, the following might be suggested. There are now a very broadly shared assumptions about the importance of attempting to measure the effectiveness and performance of local government services. Attitudes may be different in different councils and different parties and policy initiatives may be different, but there is a very clear recognition amongst members that they are increasingly moving toward establishing arrangements that allow them to review aspects of council activity at a strategic level and ask 'why' the council is doing something and to what purpose, rather than merely whether it can be done more cheaply – or not done at all. That approach to assessing performance has now become so entrenched in commonsense practice as to be almost value-free and not for political debate and argument. Labour Strathclyde wants to ensure arrangements that allow members and senior managers to assess the performance of departments and the quality of service delivery. Liberal Democrat/Labour controlled Berkshire makes provision in its management budget 'to enable the Council to continue improving efficiency and effectiveness' (Berkshire, 1992). In its annual report, Conservative-controlled Croydon provides detailed statistics on comparison with other London local authorities which will 'enable Community Charge payers and businesses to assess Croydon's performance and efficiency in delivering services' (Croydon, 1992). Croydon also provides in that same annual report a cautionary note for those who wish to assess council performance on a comparative basis. 'Care should be taken, however, in interpreting the figures. No two authorities are the same in terms of population, the problems they face or the services they provide. Furthermore, most available statistics relate only to the cost of a particular service; it is not so easy to measure service quality' (p. 4). It is also clear that helping members understand and analyse this complexity of figures provides considerable difficulties for the centre of the organisation.

In 1992 the government attempted to find ways of helping the public to measure that comparative service quality through another Local Government Act (1992). This required the Audit Commission for England and Wales and the Local Authority Accounts Commission for Scotland to direct councils to publish selected performance indicators, which it was claimed would promote the accountability of local government and help the public to assess the performance of their local authority. The next section of this chapter examines how performance indicators have become an important part of current management processes in local government.

Performance indicators – background and reality

It is perhaps an inescapable element of any discussion about 'performance' that we first strive to find ways of measuring that performance and subsequently seek to compare any measurement of performance against other comparable individuals or organisations. Unfortunately, in most aspects of our lives, it may be a chimera to imagine that we can ever satisfactorily do either of these things. An athlete wins a race and breaks a world record, yet is subsequently shown to have taken performance-enhancing drugs. The display advertisements on the financial pages contain advertisements for investment products that demonstrate how much more successful they are than their competitors – on the criteria chosen by the advertiser. Another advertisement will show the competitors to be more successful – on their chosen criteria. Despite all the available evidence suggesting it is very difficult – if not impossible – to agree clear and unambiguous measures of achievement and then to compare on the basis of these, from the early 1980s onward the government has become increasingly keen to try to do so. This has been despite the warning of even Conservative members of parliament. 'There is no acceptable scientific way of measuring efficiency as between different councils. The government thinks there is, but there isn't' (Hugh Dykes, MP, 1990).

One of the favoured methods the government has employed to attempt to do this has been to require, encourage and cajole a variety of public organisations into compiling and publishing performance indicators as a quantitative means of achievement and performance. The main aims of the Financial Management Initiative – cited above – showed an intention to 'wherever possible, measure output or performance'. Thus a requirement on central government organisations to demonstrate appropriate performance indicators in accounts of their activity. In the health service, similarly, from the early 1980s there has been a considerable investment of time and management effort put in attempting to define performance indicators for health-care and treatment.

What are performance indicators?

A number of alternative definitions have been employed by various writers; there is however a common form of words found in many government publications, and it seems perhaps most appropriate to focus upon that. The following definition is taken from a report by Her Majesty's Inspectors examining further education in Scotland (HM Government, 1990b): 'a performance indicator is a statement, often quantitative, about resources deployed and/or services provided in areas relevant to the particular objectives of the college' (p. 3). The inherent dilemma to be found in attempting to measure performance is typified by this publication. The document itself is called *Measuring Up*: which implies some absolute values, but has the subtitle 'Performance *Indicators* in Further Education' (added emphasis), suggesting that the authors themselves obviously share an understandable reluctance to attach definitive values to any of the processes they propose. They also quote approvingly a comment from a university report which urges that the emphasis should be on 'indicators as guides or signals rather than as absolute measures'. This passage continues in a similar vein to explain that 'because no single indicator is a perfect instrument and because each one is limited in its scope it is essential that a *range* of performance indicators be employed' (emphasis in original, p. 3).

So here is the dilemma, and a dilemma that faces all those who manage public services. Performance certainly seems to reflect effective management, and it is indisputably common sense and correct to attempt to measure this, but there is no absolute and unequivocally accurate way of doing so. The extracts cited above also give an indication of some of the ways in which we might address this particular problem. The first is that if we are to use performance indicators, then we should use a number of them rather than focusing on a simple 'acid ratio' as if we were assessing the immediate financial health of a trading company. The other aspect is for the council always to emphasise that these are performance *indicators* and not *measures*. A powerful analogy used by Carter *et al.* (1991) is to suggest that such indicators can be viewed as either 'dial type' or 'tin-opener type'. The argue that a preference for either of these types of indicator will indicate a particular management style and organisational setting. One might equally suggest that it is important for an organisation to have both 'dial figures' – housing applications last year, for instance – although, unless we use a 'tin opener' to examine those figures it will not necessarily help us to understand why more people (or fewer people) applied for housing. The government and the two official audit bodies have generally placed emphasis on the dial type of indicator – simple measurement. If all that local authorities do is produce the figures of measurement they are required to do then they will be wasting an opportunity to explore more vigorously the way in which the organisation performs. Examination of a variety of different approaches to assessing performance would suggest that we need to be cautious about a number of different features of employing performance indicators within an organisation. We have to think about the pitfalls we should try to avoid, and considerations we should take into account, in trying to establish an effective approach to the use of performance indicators within each council. The following considerations will be relevant to thinking about this in particular services:

- Councils should avoid just measuring that which is easily measured. The figures arrived at may not be the most useful, they may be deceptive, and they may simply give an illusion of activity. In some cases, however, the quality of even basic management information is so poor that even measuring the easy might be a reasonable starting point.

- The process of review needs to be as simple as is possible whilst still attempting to assess a range of indicators and performance. Too many organisations overburden themselves with collecting a vast array of data, the complexity of which is such that it is never transformed from data into useful information. It is also important for those who are subject to the assessment of performance to feel that they gain some advantage from the process. If they do not, then some of the worst and most negative features of time-and-motion and organisation-and-methods studies are replicated. Managers and staff should not feel that they are being spied upon, but should see some value and benefit for their work in any programme of performance measurement within the council.

- Performance indicators should relate to the 'stated objectives of the organisation' – the phrase drawn from the HMI report on further education cited above. This observation may seem self-evident, but one major area of difficulty for a manager developing performance indicators for some aspects of the work of a council is that there may be many different objectives, either formally expressed by the organisation itself or anticipated by the wide variety of different stakeholders within the organisation. So, for example, there is now an official requirement for planning departments in Scotland to publish details of the percentage of house-holder applications dealt with within given time scales, the percentage of other applications dealt with within the statutory eight-week period, and the percentage of applications approved which depart from the statutory plan. Apart from the technical debate about the validity of some of these requirements, any local authority planning department will generally recognise itself to have a far wider range of responsibilities and objectives than approving planning applications received – important as that may be.

- A significant danger that arises if the chosen performance indicators focus upon one particular aspect of the work of the organisation is that this aspect will receive more attention from staff and managers. The signal they will be given – and would be foolish to ignore – is that this is *more* important. This will be particularly important in those services and functions – planning, environmental services, trading standards, licensing, building control – where the service mix is a combination of regulatory responsibilities and developmental activities. The emphasis of the statutory performance indicators is on the former, and that is what the department will concentrate on.

- A related phenomenon and one that will cause concern to anybody thinking about performance indicators is the danger that those involved in the process will, to use a phrase much bandied around in the discussion of curriculum and assessment that has taken place in English education, 'teach to the test'. This is slightly different from the phenomenon referred to immediately above, where the strategic and departmental objectives are shifted towards those activities where there is a requirement for performance indicators to be produced and compared. The suggestion here is that within the framework created for establishing performance indicators for different functions and activities there will be a temptation to skew performance in different activities to match a profile of performance assessment that is related to those activities. So, if what is considered important about the flow of planning applications dealt with by a planning authority is the amount of time that is taken to process them then there is the danger that that time consideration may become more important than the quality of any decision related to that application. Similarly, a concern to improve the quality of front-line performance has in many councils translated into a nearly obsessional attempt to reduce telephone answering times to the shortest possible period. Far broader considerations than the time taken to respond to a telephone are important for thinking about how the council deals with the public – as is discussed in the next chapter – but this effort can be easily set aside in favour of measuring the time of a phone response.

- It is also important to try to ensure that the chosen performance indicators are unambiguous and credible. In effect, we should be trying to focus the debate on the outcome of any form of measurement, rather than the unit or form of measurement itself. A frequent rallying-call among those who are uncomfortable with or opposed to the idea of performance being assessed is: 'they're measuring the wrong thing'. Such a response may well be a case of opponents shifting the nature of opposition onto the technical process employed, but it may equally well be a genuine and valid observation on poorly designed indicators. The major apparent attraction of 'dial' type indicators is that the room for argument about their possible ambiguity is very limited; staff in the social-work inspection unit have made X number of visits to residential and daycare premises in a year. If however we try and establish how effective those visits are, we can see enormous potential for ambiguity and argument. The inspectors may feel that they have carried out an effective visit by establishing that there have been a certain number of breaches in conditions or regulations. Those being inspected (whether in local authority facilities or private) may well feel that the inspectors concern could have been more helpful in establishing the parameters of the acceptable rather than meticulously recording the unacceptable. The inherent tensions between potential ambiguity of any particular set of performance indicators further reinforces the requirement to consider a range of such indicators – but not too many.

- Creating acceptable performance indicators is also important if there is to be any comparison between individual units, between different councils. Perhaps more important for immediate management interests, there may be comparison within a particular unit or section over time. In some senses then, what we are looking for is 'benchmarks' that will enable a manager to establish some sense of direction to performance within the organisation and will also enable that manager to interpret what that direction might mean.

- This suggests another element which it will be helpful to think about in considering the implementation of a requirement to establish performance indicators and how the organisation will use them. The aimless collection of data relating to the manifold activities of any council is a pointless exercise. If performance indicators are to be established and employed usefully they should be seen as a guide to action for the council as a whole and for managers within the council. That will make it necessary for a system to be established which ensures that whatever performance indicators are designed and collected fulfil certain basis criteria. They should be available within a reasonable time-period; they should be disaggregated to a level where managers can make sense of them in both planning and operational terms; they should be accurate; but they should also be neither too few in number nor too many. All of this may seem like a counsel of perfection. It would be so if it were suggested that any organisation could move from a base of scarcely attempting to assess performance to a fully developed system of performance management in a short period. The process of effectively managing performance is something that will develop over time. It would be unwise for a council to simply adopt in an uncritical fashion the approach and systems employed by another council. Equally, although it may be necessary to acccept the imposition by an external statutory body of a requirement to publish performance indicators for particular services in particular ways, it would be unwise – and counter-productive – simply to stop at that. The actual process of developing effective approaches to performance management clearly requires time to develop, experiment, review and ensure that the process is fully accepted at significant levels within the organisation. Apart from any other factor, a more evaluative form for research – by consumer survey – for example – may show a contradiction between management data and consumer views; unhappiness with repairs, but reluctance to complain or report delay will show a low complaint record.

Observation of approaches to performance assessment in a number of public service settings would suggest that we need to stress that it takes a considerable amount of time to move beyond the easy accumulation of relatively simple data sets. Pollitt (1986) examines one local authority – Bexley – which at the time of writing was relatively advanced in employing performance assessment within the organisation. His analysis of the several hundred performance indicators cited in an annual report prepared by the council suggests that over 60 per cent of the performance indicators given related to 'efficiency' indicators; and in total 75 per cent referred to 'efficiency and economy' indicators. Only a very small percentage (1 per cent) related to effectiveness, and according to his observation none of them refers to quality of service. This seems to reinforce the point made above that measuring the easy is a start, but not enough, if we are to attempt a balanced assessment of performance within a council. The danger for many councils must be that with a statutory requirement introduced in 1993 to record and publish some performance indicators, we will leave local residents and the broader public informed only of the easily measured, without regard to those broader considerations of performance.

The statutory requirement

The Local Government Act of 1992 required the Audit Commission for England and Wales and the Commission for Local Authority Accounts in Scotland to issue directions to local authorities about the publication of performance information. The two audit bodies were required by the act to:

> give such directions as . . . [they] think fit for requiring relevant bodies to publish such information relating to their activities in any financial year as will . . . facilitate the making of appropriate comparison (by reference to the criteria of cost, economy, efficiency and effectiveness) between –

a.   the standards of performance achieved by different and relevant bodies at that financial year; and

b.   the standards of performance achieved by such bodies in different financial years (Commission for Local Authority Accounts in Scotland, 1992)

This particular aspect of the 1992 Act appeared to originate from some of the commitments given in the Citizen's Charter about public bodies demonstrating the 'standards' that they work to. Indeed, the publication by the Audit Commission which outlined its plans for developing performance indicators was entitled: *The Citizen's Charter – Local Authority Performance Indicators* (Audit Commission, 1992a). In the discussion documents issued by the two bodies as part of their consultation process each acknowledged the difficulties that were inherent in the task which they were required to carry out. As the Audit Commission observed: 'indicators must be understandable to the public, and sufficiently objective to provide valid comparisons, but without at the same time excessively simplifying the aim of the service or creating incentives to distort provision in order to perform well on a particular indicator' (p. 2).

Both bodies also acknowledge that one of the greatest difficulties is deciding which indicators should be used and how many of them there should be – something that the cautionary comments made earlier in this chapter emphasised. Both bodies carried out an extensive consultation process with local authorities and other interested bodies. The documents put out for discussion by the two separate bodies covered broadly similar ground, but there were distinct differences. The Audit Commission circulated a draft list which covered council-wide services – such as telephones – as well as many specific services. The Scottish draft did not include council wide services and excluded some specific services – such as planning – which were included in the English proposals.

In the event, the process of consultation and the decisions that flowed from that consultation produced a different response from each of the two audit bodies. The Audit Commission pruned its initial draft of more than 150 indicators covering 40 specific services to a little over 80 covering only 9 services. In Scotland, the Accounts Commission – despite having been more hesitant about an assessment of social work provision felt able to publish a direction requiring an extensive array of performance indicators related to this service.

The first list of performance indicators which local authorities were required to publish illustrates vividly the need for some form of performance assessment and simultaneously the difficulties of establishing that assessment in any way which will be generally acceptable to all those involved. It is possible to analyse the implications of this by considering some particular services more closely and comparing the published requirement from the audit bodies with the current practice of councils in a particular service. One of the strongest and most enduring municipal traditions has been a pride in creating attractive and popular urban parks. Councils as far apart – geographically and politically – as Aberdeen ('Winner of Scotland in Bloom') and Croydon ('Winner of London in Bloom') obviously attached considerable importance to those achievements. The Commission for Local Authority Accounts in Scotland will simply now require district and island councils to publish information on the 'annual cost per hectare of maintained open space' as their sole performance indicator on effective ground maintenance. Whilst it may be of technical interest to compare the actual cost of regularly running a mower across flat rectangles of grass, it is hard to see how such a figure will help local residents or visitors weigh up whether that cost is worth paying for a 'nice park' or a 'nice flower display'. In effect, the value of such a performance indicator may have some intrinsic interest but in respect of the broader considerations of this process it is of limited value. It may facilitate a comparison of cost – one of the factors which the relevant bodies were to take into account – but ignores economy, efficiency and effectiveness between authorities and over time. More broadly, we can see by looking through the list of indicators which councils are now required to publish that only limited advance has been made in the ten years since Pollitt examined the three different approaches to performance assessment. In the requirement to publish information about the local authority education service in Scotland, for example, more than two-thirds of the indicators are directly concerned with cost and economy and – depending upon fine qualification and definition – only ten are concerned with either efficiency or effectiveness.

An interesting contrast is to be found in the requirement to publish performance indicators for social work in Scotland. The initial draft proposals from the Accounts Commission were very tentative, and heavily qualified as being in only draft form. In England, the Audit Commission, despite having issued draft proposals, declined to make a formal direction on the publication of social services performance data.

Among the variety of performance indicators that social work departments in Scotland are now required to publish, only in a minority of instances is financial information – on spending or costs – requested. There is some emphasis on efficiency measures, through a requirement to estimate the total number of persons that may fall into different categories of care within a community care plan and the number that had been assessed in the past year. A considerable proportion of the performance indicators required make a very good attempt to establish some criteria for the *effectiveness* or *quality* of service. So, for example, authorities are required to report on the proportion of children in care living in 'homely settings', and the proportion of various residential staffs who are qualified. They also have to show the proportion of residential care places across all three sectors in which the children, offenders, elderly people, or other adults have a private room. It may be that such directions will provide fruitful material for a debate within the social work profession about whether such indicators are an appropriate set of criteria for assessing effective performance, but those professionals can hardly complain about an excessive concentration on cost and expenditure. This also provides an instructive contrast with the range of performance data currently published by local authorities in their annual reports. The London Borough of Croydon (Annual Report 1991/92) and Durham County Council (Annual Report 1990/91) give, respectively, eight and eleven performance indicators, with comparable statistics for similar authorities. In the first case three of the eight refer to overall client cost figures; and in Durham four of the eleven do so.

Both audit bodies have already indicated that they will review the first year's experience of requiring the publication of a standardised set of performance indicators for different services; and will extend, adapt or change the arrangements they have made. The evidence provided here does not lead to a clear view of how that process will develop. However, what is suggested is that in an emergent system there is considerable scope for practitioners and managers in the field to help shape debate about the form that that system may finally take. If that is to occur, managers will need to consider carefully how they adapt and employ at a local level the processes involved in managing performance.

What should the manager do?

Quite clearly both senior managers and the council as a whole will have an obligation to compile the necessary data which will allow the publication of required performance indicators in the annual report and elsewhere. If all the authority and its managers do is no more than that, then essentially the exercise will be a sterile and ritualistic one. The effective and sensitive use of a range of appropriate performance indicators can be helpful both to the organisation and to its managers. It can aid the development and adaptation of services and facilities in a way which is intended to improve quality and more readily meet the needs of service-users.

The starting point will be to ensure that data is collected in a fashion which enables it to be aggregated for all council purposes and disaggregated for the purposes of local comparison and decision-making. If all the required information tells us is the proportion of pupils in the first year of primary education with experience of education department preschooling – and assesses that against the target for such pupils and the target for other forms of preschool education, then the information will be interesting. It will become far more interesting for members and managers and serve as a far more valuable guide to practice and service development – if the information is available on the basis of definition by different parts of the authority. So, in the largest authorities, such information will need to be by division or district; in the smaller authorities, by neighbourhood or community.

It will also be helpful for a manager to develop additional performance indicators which are more closely tailored to the immediate requirements of a particular service and the context in which it is delivered. Ideally these should be developed in consultation with staff and users. We might seek to establish, for example, a better understanding of the requirements that particular users of a service have – and for that matter an understanding of who the non-users are and why they are non-users of a particular service. It is not unduly difficult to develop a lot of performance factors for a particular activity or service; it is difficult if we either concentrate obsessional energy on 'getting it right' or invest an absolute reliance upon them as a definitive statement of performance. A recognition that the use of performance indicators is intrinsically an iterative process would be helpful. If we were to acknowledge that, the way would be cleared to recognise that after the first year, alternative approaches to assessing effectiveness will emerge and the manner in which we do this will be superseded by more sophisticated approaches which can perhaps take broader account of hitherto neglected stakeholders within the organisational process.

There are two good examples of this in the education field. Strathclyde Region has done pioneering work in analysing the available data for school performance far more closely to establish which of its secondary schools do more to add value in the educational process. Thus, for example, it is entirely possible for a school which apparently achieves poor public examination results to have provided a more effective education for those who attend it than a school with perhaps a more privileged catchment area and intake. Similarly, 'the *Guardian*' has consistently championed a programme of attempting to assess the comparable added value for 'A'-level examination results in England and Wales. Both approaches have taken on and developed a better understanding of what we might look for when we consider how schools contribute to young people's educational achievement.

As with so many of the other changes which are currently affecting the management of local government, the management technology is not as daunting as it first appears. Such processes and approaches are being developed and adapted by managers in many local authorities throughout Britain. The major shift that is required within organisations is a recognition by members, chief officers, and managers throughout the council that now and for the foreseeable future they will be required to think in terms of the performance of the unit and the organisation, and to demonstrate the effectiveness of that performance. They will have to demonstrate that effectiveness both to external monitoring agencies, and to the most important people for any council – the residents, users and consumers of local government services.

Some points for discussion

1. Do you think it is possible to measure performance in local government services?
2. Who should set standards for performance? Professionals? Politicians? Service users?
3. How effective are public organisations at sticking to their own performance criteria?
4. Can performance comparison be a substitute for competition?
5. What should the public, the council and the government do about persistent underperformance?

8   Users and Consumers

Most of the action in the play *On the Ledge* by Alan Bleasdale (1993) is set outside the upper floors of a tower block. Various characters are either considering suicide or find themselves trapped there for other reasons. Moey, an exasperated firefighter, is trying to rescue them and gradually loosing his patience with their unwillingness to be rescued. There is an exchange of dialogue between one of those on the ledge and the firefighter.

> *Mal*: 'you could try a little charm. . .'
> *Moey*: 'I couldn't do that, I work with the public. . .'

He subsequently goes on to vent his rage at various individual members and groups within the broader society, to the great amusement of the audience. The play is a farce, and the action is intended to be humorous, but for those who work in local government that exchange has a serious point. The fire service is probably among those local government services most highly regarded by the general public; firefighters are seen as professional, competent, and brave. The frustration expressed by Moey could perhaps be seen as the broader frustration of such committed professionals working in a service where they have a very clear idea of what they should be doing, and yet suddenly coming to realise that in a changing world people do not necessarily *want* the service that they are providing so effectively and competently. In this case the people trapped on a high ledge of a building did not want to be rescued, elsewhere residents do not agree with the planning department proposals for their community, or a family isn't happy with what social workers plan for their grandmother. Across a wide range of local government services victims, clients, users, customers, and residents are increasingly deciding that they are not willing to operate on the general assumption that 'the council knows best'.

It is not simply in local government, but in many other public services, that we have seen a major change in the relationship that people assume they have with such large organisations. That change is expressed in different ways depending on the nature of the organisation and the service or product it provides, but whereever we look we are able to find evidence that the users and consumers (or whatever we decide to call them) are – when they are in a position to do so – seeking to establish a new relationship with the organisations that provide for them.

Adjusting to this has not been easy for organisations in many different sectors of the economy. Plenty of businesses have declined and collapsed because they did not adjust quickly enough to the changing taste of consumers and purchasers. Many public organisations find it exceptionally difficult to develop an appropriate model of a relationship between them and the people whom they serve. There is a considerable ambivalence in the attitude of those who run such services, which is often expressed in their grappling for the appropriate term to describe the people with whom they deal – inparticular those people to whom they provide a service. It is perhaps understandable that British Telecom – now an international communications PLC – should refer to its 'customers', and British Rail has also increasingly taken to referring to passengers as 'customers'. In other areas of the public service a changed vocabulary is seen to presage a different relationship between the provider and the recipient. On his appointment as chief executive of the Benefits Agency, the former chief executive of Gloucestershire County Council, Mike Bichard was interviewed on the radio for *Today* programme. He expressed his view that: 'I think it is more than a token change, I think it is very important to the way in which you treat people and frankly if you call people claimants I think you treat them in a particular way – customers is the word we want to use' (Bichard, 1991)

In local government, there has been for some years an uncomfortable hesitancy about simply adopting the word 'customer' as a means of providing a helpful perspective for the organisation. The local government correspondent of the *Scotsman* was clearly not comfortable with this when he referred to: 'Labour's policy on the provision of services has a strong emphasis on quality and the rights of consumers and customers – words that are now the modern way of describing the people councillors represent' (Scott, 1990). Among local authorities there are clearly mixed views. Watford in a 1992 job advertisement describes its core values as: Citizens, Customers, Quality, Equality, People, Poverty and Environment. Elsewhere, shortly after his appointment as chief executive, David Henshaw of Knowsley rather confusingly described the word 'customer' as 'a bit passé' (Rosenthal, 1991). The point to be emphasised is the extent to which a changing perception of the way in which local government relates to the consumer of services has also brought into question the very vocabulary used to describe those consumers. The uncertainty that can arise from this and the degree to which it can cause confusion within the organisation can be seen in a publication by the National Consumer Council which examines services in different councils. In the foreword the chairman of the NCC uses the term 'customers', but that word is not used at all in the subsequent forty or fifty pages of the report (National Consumer Council, 1986). The purpose of this chapter is to examine the dilemmas that local authorities and local authority managers must face when they consider the people for whom they are providing services. It also examines the ways in which the nature of the relationship between the organisation and those people has changed and is changing, and considers the implications of that for managing the organisation.

Citizens or customers?

In mid-1991 the prime minister launched a White Paper, *The Citizen's Charter*. His foreword to the document expressed in very personal terms the themes of the documents: 'I take great pleasure in the first set of initiatives under the Citizen's Charter. To make public services answer better to the wishes of their users, and to raise their quality overall, have been ambitions of mine ever since I was a local Councillor in Lambeth over twenty years ago' (p. 2). The proposals contained in the initial document were broadly welcomed, though sometimes in a rather backhanded fashion. *The Economist* (1991, p. 23) claimed that: 'John Major's Citizen's Charter is easy to ridicule. For a start it is a customer's charter, not a citizen's. It is also a slick re-packaging of old policies, with touches of originality restricted for the most part to ideas like making hitherto – anonymous public servants wear name badges' (p. 23). The weekly went on to observe, acutely, that the impetus to improve quality in public services would best be achieved by two main pressures consistently referred to in the proposals – targets and monitoring, and competition and privatisation. Whilst other political parties were critical of the government's launch of the Charter, that criticism was often expressed in terms of claiming earlier and more wholehearted support for many of the ideas contained in the Charter. Indeed, much of the energy put into discussion about the government document was based upon the opposition representatives' claim that, whilst many of the ideas were all very good, their party had actually had them first and where they had any opportunity to do so had been putting them into effect.

An earlier theme in this book has been the extent to which many of the ideas which now inform and drive our approaches to managing public services are shared broadly across the party spectrum. Reaction to the Citizen's Charter would seem to confirm this. By and large, and with the possible exception of those parts of the document that emphasise competitive tendering and market testing, the ideas contained within the White Paper were viewed as relatively unexceptional, quite commendable, and to be found already in place in many local authorities controlled by either the Labour Party or the Liberal Democrats or both jointly. The extent to which the variety of approaches described in the charter proposals reflect a convergent trend of managerial thinking about public services has been illustrated by those ministers responsible for overseeing public services. In an interview with the Open University, Robert Jackson MP, parliamentary secretary to the Office of Public Service and Science, referred to the Citizen's Charter as 'total quality management for the public sector' (Open University, 1993). Secretary of State William Waldegrave indicated to members of a parliamentary committee that he sees a major part of his task as the 'bringing together of various strands of public service reform and emphasising the coherence of those different strands' (House of Commons, 1993). Those major strands of public sector reform have been characterised by this government as placing increasing emphasis on improving opportunities for individual choice. If there is a distinction between government and opposition it is perhaps that the Conservative Party is brought to this view by a disposition to favour an increase in individual choice, whereas the opposition parties have been forced to recognise that more and more people expect increased opportunities for individual choice. Increasing numbers of people consider themselves to have that choice available to them in the trading sector, and therefore expect it to be available in public services as well. Writing in *The Guardian* in (1988), Jack Straw MP, who later became shadow environment secretary, claimed that: 'We must recognise that a nation of consumers, enjoying relatively high living standards, becomes literally much more choosy, much more interested in choice and variety. . .. The aspirations of choice are spreading from consumer goods to public services, and rightly so' (Straw, 1988). Whether individuals have that increased choice in the trading sector is both a matter of circumstance and perhaps as much as anything of perception; however, one of the most important lessons for those in the public services to learn is that perception of service, of quality and availability is important in helping individuals form a judgement about the nature of the organisation that is providing for them.

There is in this a considerable and as yet unresolved difficulty for those parties which favour the collective provision of services and facilities for the community. The increased opportunity to express individual choice, and the consequences that flow from that, which may include competition between providers, can have long-term and undesirable consequences. If we all as consumers have increased individual choice, and choose one from between two or more alternative providers, then if the majority of us opt for the same thing some will be frustrated in not getting their choice. At the same time, other providing institutions will continue to decline as users walk away from them. So in many areas, the programmes of school closure and amalgamation which local authorities have been required to pursue have followed not simply from an overall decline in potential pupil numbers but have been exacerbated by a flight from particular institutions. This may throw into disarray broader patterns of strategic choice within the council. In a report for Strathclyde Regional Council on the organisation of its education department, Inlogov (1989) highlighted this dilemma: 'There is a potential conflict between the strategies of local and central government which present the Education Service in Strathclyde with a dilemma: can it reconcile the Authorities' emphasis upon *community* development within the social strategy with the Government's legislative programme that strives to strengthen the *consumer* and the institution: possibly at the expense of the authority' (p. 10). In a discussion on a proposed programme of school closures, the convener of an education committee expressed this difficulty even more bluntly by observing that the reason the school was closing was because the majority of the parents who lived within the catchment area chose not to send their children there; *they* had made the choice about the future of the school, not the education committee (private interview).

Many councils recognise this delicate balance between the individual and the community, the consumer and the citizen, and try to work out their own way of balancing the demands and pressures that arise from the existence of a variety of stakeholders in a council with a broader concern for the political expression of community. Leicester City Council has produced a 'council charter' which indicates the council: 'exists to ensure that local services and the environment reach the highest possible standards within the resources available for citizens, visitors and those who work in the city' (Leicester, n.d.). The council also specifically provided advice for employees on the different ways – in person, in writing, on the phone, and visiting them at home – to treat people who come into contact with the council as though they were customers. York City Council was one of the first councils to develop the idea of a local charter, and it recognised the dangers of placing too much emphasis on residents as solely the consumers of services. This can create a very one-dimensional picture of what the local authority should see itself as responsible for. A report on progress in York (Wills, 1991) quotes one senior official as recognising: 'There is a danger that just relying on the customer agenda plays to much into the line: the private sector knows best . . . the council is not just about providing services but creating a lively local democracy.'

If a council is to attempt to get this balance right, it must examine carefully the different relationships it has with both different members of the public and different publics. So, for example, the occasional user of a sports facility will have a very different view of the council from somebody who lives in a local authority house on a local authority estate surrounded by facilities which are entirely in the ownership and control of one or more councils. Equally – as the extract above from the Leicester charter implies – there is a distinction between those who live in a community and those who visit that community. They have different requirements, different attitudes and different rights. These different rights may be expressed in different ways: the visitor cannot vote, and most visitors appear not to be offended at the idea that they may pay more at the door for some facilities than would local residents. In developing an analysis of whom they are to serve and how they are to serve them, it becomes important for council managers to understand exactly why the consumer of many council services cannot be treated just like a customer, who if not keen on the goods in one shop can walk to the shop next door. Clearly the relationship and the perspective that an individual will have on the organisation will vary from service to service (between swimming pool and local authority tenancy). There are however certain characteristics which distinguish the consumer of many local authorities' services from the customer buying in a shop or restaurant:

- The consumers of many public services have no choice in their consumption. This is either because they are compelled to accept the service – as is a child taken into care – or they are within a jurisdiction in which there is only one provider. So, if a resident wishes to apply for planning consent to extend a property, it is not possible to opt for a consent given by officials of the neighbouring council on the grounds that they are more sympathetic to house extension or modern design. The resident concerned can try to persuade the local council to change its policies or to make an exception in an individual case, but must nonetheless live with the decisions of that particular regulatory regime.

- Many users of public services have no choice because they have no means of acquiring that alternative – they are constrained by geographic immobility and must use the local old swimming pool rather than the modern leisure pool because that is located further away and they have no car. They may rent a house from the local authority because they do not have the means to buy. They may even be physically constrained because of distance and location from exercising any of the choices notionally made available to them by recent changes in legislation. It is not a coincidence that the pressure for parental choice for school places has been most pronounced in urban areas, rather than in the more remote rural areas where a thirty- or forty-mile journey for children to attend an alternative secondary school is not really an option.

- Economic theory says that all resources are scarce. In a purchasing relationship, with a queue of customers willing and able to pay, the provider will be encouraged to reinvest and provide more stocks in order to meet increased demand. The public manager faced with increased demand may well have to ration, and find ways to restrict that demand because no more funding is available for that particular service. Typically the solution is either to put a cap on entering (as with school places), or to make the criteria for access more rigorous – as with the allocation of aids for the physically handicapped. Whatever the course of action taken by the manager the net effect is to create a queue which will ration such services.

- In the case of many public services, the process is in effect the product. The consumer of the service is not simply buying a one-off item such as a pair of socks, but is engaging in a long-term relationship with, perhaps, a teacher, a social worker, doctor or other comparable professional. The quality of the service and the way in which that is perceived by the consumer will be influenced by many factors – not all of which necessarily imply an immediate and correct solution to a particular problem but all of which contribute to building a long-term relationship. When that relationship breaks down, the individual cannot simply walk into another shop, but will expect that the public agency or the government as supervisor of that public agency will take necessary and often complex steps to rebuild that relationship. So, the response to any such incident – certainly of a major type – is often seen to be in the form of a major enquiry and the re-shaping of policies and procedures on a universal basis – e.g the Cleveland Enquiry and the Allitt Child Murder Enquiry.

To summarise, what is being argued here is that public organisations, and in particular local government, cannot simply view their relationship with the public as being that of provider to customer. They must analyse and keep in balance the appropriate relationships with and approaches to the different publics whom the council serves. If they are not able to do this then they find themselves caught in the trap described by a senior officer in the Metropolitan Police in an article on the changing police force. The writer indicated how the former commissioner had developed his ideas for a what he called 'a customer-orientated service', rather than a produce-driven force. ' "We took our lessons from the gurus of British Airways and British Telecom, but then we adapted it to a police force" ', Marnoch says' (Sweeting, 1993). Unfortunately, as the author observed in his article, whilst the profits and performance of those two companies proved variable over time the performance of the Metropolitan Police and its public perception appeared to continue on a steady long-term downward trend. For councils to get the balance right they need to develop different approaches to thinking about individuals within the community both as consumers of services – 'customers' – and as citizens who have a broader and political interest in the operation of their council. The next two sections of this chapter examine the implications of those two different perspectives for local managers.

The citizen as consumer

Because of the pressures that have arisen from a variety of social and economic changes in recent years, local government has been forced to think far more about the perspective of the consumer. Even if those changes had not occurred, creating a more aware, sophisticated, and discerning community, then local authorities would in any event have been required to examine the relationship between the organisation and those who benefit from the services it provides. Over and above the expectation of greater individual choice, variety and provision, and opportunity to select from alternative providers, there are other forces at work here. Both legislative change and the broader social movements which have both led and been shaped by that change now encourage us to think far more about the rights we have as consumers of goods and services of all kinds. Whilst we may not always be overly well informed about those rights, they are nonetheless available to us and are built around a programme of action which has been broadly represented by a consumer movement both here and in other industrialised countries.

There are several key strands comprising the consumer approach to services and products. In each case it is possible to see the manner in which each of these strands has either been taken up in the management of local government services or – conversely – is still neglected. The main elements which define this approach to consumerism are usually described in the following terms (Beishon, 1989). There should be access to the services and goods that people want, in the appropriate place at the right time.

Increasing numbers of local authorities are adopting a far more sophisticated approach to planning the location of facilities, and the delivery and timing of services. Such planning should take into account the particular interests and needs of those who already do use the services or may become the users of them:

- Is there a range of choices available to the consumer? In some respects it is in this aspect of provision that local authorities have been forced to make organisational change by central government legislation. In schools and housing in particular – services which have been central to the lives of many millions of families – councils were not, until recently, good at making choice available to those who wanted such choice. Nonetheless in those services, and since 1993 in some aspects of community-care provision, there is going to be a requirement on local authorities to extend the range of choices available to individuals and families.

- There should be good information available to a potential consumer of products or services. There has been a dramatic improvement in recent years in the variety of information made available to service-users. Not only has the range of information improved but so has the quality of that information and the way in which it is presented. Changing media technologies have helped here, with access to quality printing rather than the traditional duplicated A4 sheet.

- Does the consumer have access to redress if things go wrong? This has been a long-standing element in consumer demands, but does present a particular difficulty for both the users and the providers of public services. At one extreme can be the dramatic and tragic – can there ever be redress for the bungled operation that takes or ruins a life? Equally, if our train is late and we miss an important interview does a free ticket or compensation of five pounds provide any solace? This is not solely a difficulty for the public sector; there are few things more unappealing than the offer of a free meal at the restaurant where you contracted food poisoning! More seriously it is noticeable that only recently have some authorities appeared to develop their own internal approaches to handling complaints about misapplied procedures and inappropriate decisions. Indeed there was for some years a strong undercurrent of resistance to and resentment about the powers of the respective commissioners for local administration (Ombudsmen). Similarly, in many local authorities it is possible to get a clear message of resistance to any attempt to challenge the prerogative of the council to make the final decision on matters within its jurisdiction. It is not easy to develop approaches to creating effective redress for individuals; it is however important and it is one area in which local government still has much progress to make.

- A requirement that the product or service should be safe. Whilst this may at first appear to be more relevant to the seller of a dangerous car or a poorly designed child's toy, if we think in broader terms than simply the immediate danger of a physical accident then such a principle clearly does have relevance to local authority services. There are – regrettably – still many housing authorities letting properties to tenants which may pose short- or even long-term health risk to them and their families. Judging the fine balance between making housing available and making housing habitable and decent is a difficult choice for any public provider to make; it is however not always clear that the councils concerned err on the side of the health and safety of the potential tenant.

- If we take account of the position of a broad cross-section of consumers then it will also be necessary to consider whether the form of service provision is fair across the range of those who are or may potentially be consumers. This is particularly significant for publicly funded and publicly accountable organisations which are meant to deal equitably with those who are potentially eligible to benefit from a particular service. For trading organisations, considerations of fairness are in some ways both more simple and more complex. So, for example, the car insurance company which refuses business from certain types of people – typically young males who wish to drive high-performance theft-attractive cars – would reasonably claim it is being fair to other motorists. Fortuitously for the company, such an approach to business also helps to produce impressive profit figures. For a local authority the choice may be far more difficult and the appropriate cost of action far less clear. Many teachers will observe, on the basis of empirical evidence, that the quality of classroom interaction and the quality of education provided to the majority of their fourteen- fifteen- and sixteen-year-old pupils would be far better if they didn't have to cope with three or four uninterested and truculent young male teenagers who also have a place in class. The parents of those three or four young men, and all those with a broader interest in the educational opportunities provided to the young within that community, would reasonably argue that removing them would have many drawbacks and may be unacceptable. The challenge for a democratically representative and accountable public organisation is how, in such circumstances, it may reconcile the needs and interests of the majority against the needs of the minority.

- The final strand of the consumer argument – representation – is arguably taken better account of in the public sector than in the private. Consumers do not have access to the decision-making centres of large trading organisations. In local government, there is of course the representation of democratically elected members – a representative role which we shall return to below. Equally, in many authorities there are imaginative and bold attempts made to ensure more successful user representation and to find ways of creating an effective network of community representation at appropriate decision-making levels, to balance and complement the views of directly elected members.

If local authorities are to ensure that their services, facilities and procedures effectively meet the appropriate criteria of achievement under those different elements of the consumer perspective, then they will need to test out many aspects of their activity against them. It is also, however, important for councils to recognise that the people whom they serve do not merely present themselves to the organisation as consumers but also as citizens with a broader social and political interest in the community and in the organisation which is elected to serve that community. The final aspect referred to in considering the perspective of the consumer was that of representation: that is a useful starting point from which to consider the other face of the various publics whom a council must consider.

The consumer as citizen

One major omission in much current discussion about improving the management of local government is a lack of reference to the rights and duties of men and women as citizens of a parliamentary democracy with universal suffrage. Despite the grand title of '*The Citizen's Charter*', numerous commentators have observed that it actually pays little attention to the individual rights of a citizen or of the possible ways in which citizens collectively might see their rights enhanced. The very word 'citizen' must actually be an uncomfortable word for a Conservative government to use. It does not fit well into the public vocabulary of contemporary Britain, and for some Conservatives must be curiously redolent of the remembered horrors of the French Revolution. The current emphasis of much discussion on rights, and the manner in which that has often been applied to local government, has tended to devalue the concept of citizenship and emphasise the role of the individual – or the family – as a consumer or customer. It is however important that when analysing the management of our public services and attempting to improve that management we have a clear idea of the relationship between the customer and the citizen; without that, one cannot effectively answer the various demands that will be placed upon the organisation by individuals, families and communities through the different perspectives they may have in those different roles. The two roles clearly interact because, for political institutions, whilst getting it right for the customer is important, the ultimate democratic accountability is to people as citizens. As *The Economist* (1991, p. 24) sharply observed on the launch of the Citizen's Charter: 'That will not save the Tories if the Charter turns out in the end to be no more than fine intentions.'

It has been argued in other chapters that a number of trends in our current thinking about improving the quality of management in local government owe much to ideas that have been developed within the private sector and translated – sometimes transplanted – into the public services. As discussed above, one other powerful element of this is the concentration that good organisations apparently give to 'the customer'. The originators of the 'excellence' school of management, Peters and Waterman (1982), described the organisations they observed as being 'obsessive' about customers. Many local government managers have clearly been very heavily influenced by the ideas contained in this book, and subsequent such books. The influence of these ideas on British local government have been significantly advanced through the work of Michael Clarke and John Stewart, who over several years and through a variety of books and papers have encouraged the evolution of what they have called the 'public service orientation – PSO' (Clarke and Stewart, 1985 etc.). The central case they have put forward is that 'local authorities' activities exist to provide services for the public', and they go on to argue that councils will be judged by the quality of service provided within the resources which the council has, and the value of the service can best be judged from the point of view of those to whom it is provided. They further claim that the people receiving services are customers who want high-quality services, and in order to develop high-quality services it is important to be 'close to the customer'. When this argument was first launched in the United Kingdom it represented a powerful and refreshing blast of change, essentially arguing that local authorities should pay a lot more attention to those who receive a service rather than concentrate energies on the internal requirements and demands of the organisation. In subsequent papers and articles (Clarke and Stewart, 1986a; Clarke and Stewart, 1986b) the two authors emphasised that the consumers of public services cannot be seen in the same way as purchasers in a retail store, and that the council must see them as both citizens *and* consumers of a service. 'The PSO focuses on the customer *and the citizen*; it cannot ignore that the customer is also a citizen or that there are citizens other than the customer' (1986b, p. 2). In subsequent work (1990a), Clarke and Stewart have gone on to make the duality role of customer and citizen far more explicit. Nonetheless, it is not unreasonable to suggest that the initial powerful influence of their joint work was to emphasise the role of customer over that of citizen, and to do so by overly stressing the function and the responsibility of the council to provide services, rather than seeing its function as a form of local self-government.

This emphasis is not surprising; from the immediate point of view of most people, the most important thing a council does is to provide an array of different services. Indeed, for many people it would sometimes appear that the intrusion of 'party politics' into that process is at best unfortunate and at worst highly undesirable. More widely, it is important for the health of the democratic process that local authorities should continue to develop strategies which seek to combine the interests of people as consumers with those of people as citizens. Since a number of councils are already moving in this direction, it is now possible for us to see this as part of a longer term pattern of change within the organisation of local government. Historically many councils – whether Labour, Conservative, Liberal or non-party – had an tradition of central control and paternalistic practices. Local government in the cities was often controlled by powerful political bosses, and in the counties by local notables. In the 1960s, as broad social changes occurred, many councils discovered a popular reaction against traditional patterns of decision-making. Local authorities which had previously torn down acres of housing, either for rebuilding or for road programmes, suddenly found their proposals vigorously challenged by people unpersuaded that the council knew best and asserting their rights as citizens, unwilling to accept that those rights should be confined to an occasional election. In government, the minister of housing and local government established a committee to review planning practices. Chaired by a thoroughly conventional Labour parliamentary secretary, the committee report, 'People and Planning', was published in 1969 (Skeffington, 1969). Tony Benn, another more senior minister in that same government, also found his views changing, and he came to think that there should be more public participation in the decision-making of various institutions. So there was a process of change in which various elements advanced claims for greater measures of popular participation. It is important to recall how unpopular many of these ideas were. Skeffington was booed and jeered at a Labour Party local government conference; Benn was dubbed by his critics (many of whom were his colleagues) as 'Citizen Benn' (with the word there clearly used in a derisory sense!).

The late 1960s and the 1970s saw a varied and often erratic pattern of change, in and around the institutions and decision-making processes of local government. This ranged from squatters' unwillingness to accept homelessness, and equally unwilling to accept a council definition of empty properties as being unsuitable to live in. Elsewhere, individuals and communities of various degrees of privilege and politeness argued and protested against clearance and construction plans of one kind or another, whether initiated by local government (town redevelopment and housing), central government (motorways), or major utilities (power stations). From the perspective suggested here, we should add in to all these elements of collective and community activity an increasing emphasis on the rights of the individual as a consumer. The two Labour governments of the 1970s legislated for consumer rights, created the National and Scottish Consumer Councils, and established a cabinet post with responsibility for consumer affairs. In the 1980s, with a change in government and change in government thinking, there was a shift back towards the interests of the individual, which for many in those Conservative governments were best seen expressed through the influence of his or her market power. In local government, the response was, as discussed above, a concentration on the local authorities providing services and on the individual or household as a recipient of those services.

FIGURE 8.1   Changes in local councils

Central and paternalistic control
(the council as provider)

A challenge to that central power
(sections of the community reject council solutions)

The legal rights of the individual
(consumer legislation, consumer agencies, the Commissioners for
Local Administration)

The council as provider
(public services as a shop where customers choose,
concentration on services for the individual)

Citizens and consumers
(a new synthesis?)

It is possible to see in all of this a web of connections – rather than an unbroken thread – which leads as is shown in Figure 8.1. We can test out this schematic representation of change against the actual change of practice in different local authority services. Housing provides a good example. Because attitudes and practices differ so widely in different local authorities, it is not possible to put a firm chronological timescale to the changing practices which we now see in place in many housing authorities. The sequence of change would, however, generally look like this:

- Many thousands of households live in poor quality, privately rented or cheaply bought accommodation.
- Council house building programmes begin. As always, the vocabulary of practice is highly instructive. Potential tenants are not 'offered' a property but are 'allocated' one. Their response was usually delight, which was fortunate because the general assumption within the council was that people take what is given to them.
- Major rebuilding programmes begin in the centre of towns and cities. Existing tenants and in many cases owner-occupiers of low-cost, low-value housing are told that their house is 'unfit' and that when they move they will be allocated a local authority house elsewhere. Into the 1960s there was an increasing tendency for local communities to become organised and protest against such wholesale demolition. Government action and subsequently legislation encourages greater emphasis on rehabilitation of housing rather than clearance.
- Some councils introduce a more sensitive rehousing programme, which provides for people to be rehoused close to or within preexisting communities wherever possible.
- Councils introduce modernisation programmes for housing built many years earlier and do so on the basis that they will define the quality of work to be done, and the nature of work to be done on particular properties. Tenants are assumed to accept this gratefully.
- The expectations of potential local authority tenants rise, and increasing numbers of people are unwilling to accept the houses which are offered to them by the council. Within some councils there was – and still is – a reluctance to accept that potential tenants should be so ungrateful.
- In-house letting some councils develop more sensitive policies, willing to support people into a new tenancy and to attempt to find appropriate choices of accommodation for them.
- In modernisation, rehabilitation, and new building, councils develop policies that provide for extensive – and demanding – consultation with individual households and with representative bodies of tenants and community associations.

There are still many councils where it is considered improper for a potential tenant to refuse a property. He or she – despite now being a 'customer' – is not allowed the opportunity to make what may appear to be (to the council) a capricious and frivolous decision if the person concerned is to demonstrate that they are in genuine need of housing. Yet in contrast, all those of us who have ever bought properties will know that many potential properties are rejected by would-be purchasers on grounds such as including location, sunny side of the street, just plain 'look of the place'.

In summary, what is being argued is that in their dealings with the public – as individuals, as households, or as a broader community – councils have moved through a number of stages. Those stages are not clearly defined, they are not neat and tidy, and in some cases (on councils controlled by any of the parties) the council remains locked into the paternalistic, centralised and unresponsive mould of decision-making and service provision. It is important for the local government manager to first of all establish the position in the council, and then consider what approaches must be adopted to take the unit, department or council as a whole 'closer to the public', to echo the title of a handbook from the Local Government Training Board (1987).

Some action to be taken

An examination of different practices in various local authorities suggests that in practical terms there are several aspects to reshaping the organisation and making it more responsive to consumers and the community. Some of these may require an all-council approach, others can be implemented at departmental level, and yet others can be put into effect at the unit level of the operational manager. In the latter instance, it would appear that in some authorities initiatives taken within one unit or section of the department have later extended throughout the authority as a whole as examples of good practice.

The courses of action that could be taken up include the following:

- The council could examine exactly who benefits from the service or facility provided. Assumptions are often made about those who benefit from local authority services with no serious exam-ination of empirical data. Bramley (1990) examined the extent to which different forms of service provision in Cheshire are enjoyed by different types of households and different social groups. For a council that is committed to policies of redistribution and support in areas of social stress it is essential to establish exactly who is benefiting from and enjoying the service.

- They could ask people what they actually think about the service they receive. Despite the increasing popularity among local authorities of consumer and resident surveys, it is still only a minority of councils who do this. At a unit level, it is not difficult to find ways of asking people: What do they think about the swimming pool? Are the opening hours appropriate for them? What is the most convenient time for staff to call at the house? The consultancy PA completed a survey of more than two hundred local authorities in England and Wales in late 1989 and approximately 40 per cent of these systematically surveyed what the users of services thought of the services provided (*Local Government Chronicle*, 1990).

- Managers should also consider the accessibility of the service or facility for which they are responsible. This may cover aspects of physical access – convenience of location and physical accessibility of the building. It should also cover access in terms of public perception of the facility – for example, do older women view the sports centre as being somewhere where loud and rowdy young men hang out? Area-wide, the council as a whole should also consider the physical distribution of facilities and services. Access audit will often reveal a large number of areas within the community where services are sporadically or poorly distributed.

- Managers will also need to consider how much opportunity is given to the public to express a voice and a view of a service. The general trend of legislation from this government is clearly intended to extend the range of lay involvement in some public services. In some cases senior local government staff will be forced to live with this arrangement – however reluctantly. Elsewhere, it can be a fruitful development for managers to think about how they can create a more effective working and decision-making relationship that will involve the manager, the public and councillors.

All in all, there are many exciting – and sometimes disorientating – changes occurring in local government. Many of those changes are intended to make local government far more responsive to the people who walk through the doors of the swimming pool or theatre; or those who expect somebody to call at their house to fix a drainpipe or discuss a road improvement. Local government can learn a great deal from the most effective and successful of public companies – though not, as sometimes implied, from every trading concern, whether it be local market stall or multinational company. However, our interest in how well a high-street store is run ends at whether or not it can provide the goods 'I want, when I want, at the price I want' (to paraphrase a former prime minister). Our interest in a local council goes far wider than this. It is a representative institution, it is elected by universal suffrage, and it is a forum where those whom we elect make decisions about the future of our community, as well as about the number of library books and the size of a garage extension. If that council is to work more effectively in handling the multiplicity of interests of the variety of publics within the community, then we need to give serious attention to the way in which councillors are helped to do their job, because for many of the users of council services, their view of the council turns upon the performance of the local councillor.

Some points for discussion

1. Do you think the way we describe the users of public services has implications for the way they are treated?
2. Is the role of the customer more important than the role of the citizen?
3. How can local authorities be more flexible and respond to individual demands?
4. How much choice should councils provide within different services?

9 Managing Members or Members Managing?

At some point during any discussion with local government officials at least one person present will either imply – or directly claim – that 'everything would be much better if it weren't for the members'. In similar terms, those services now subject to a contractual regime will often see managers express resentment that their service must carry a part of the cost of 'the democratic process'. These same officials will, however, often assert that the authority of the council to do certain things (to impose a school rationalisation programme) or its right to do things in a certain way (the compulsory purchase of land) is justified because it is mandated by the democratic process of elections.

Such ambivalent views about the nature and legitimacy of the political process are not confined to local government officials. There would often appear to be a widely held folk myth (and myth it is) that at some earlier and unspecified date there was a golden age of local government when 'politics didn't come into it; it was just for the good of the town'. This ambivalent attitude to the politics of local government – or that aspect of politics expressed through the views and action of councillors – has also been shared at the highest levels of government. In 1985, the government announced the establishment of a committee, chaired by David Widdicombe QC, to examine 'the conduct of local authority business' (Widdicombe, 1986a). Among the reasons for establishing this committee was ministerial concern that: 'There is a cancer in some local councils which runs much deeper than extravagant spending. . . . Local democracy itself is under attack . . . officers are selected for their political views . . . the conventional checks and balances are scorned' (Quoted M. Gyford *et al.*, 1989, p. 286).

The terms of the criticism and the language itself indicate a very clear ministerial concern about what were described at the time of the committee appointment as 'abuses of power' in local government. Nonetheless, in a public speech delivered during the middle of the committee enquiry, the Secretary of State for the Environment spoke favourably about councillors taking a more direct role in the management of their councils, in terms that were actually quoted in the final report of the Widdicombe committee:

> Since 1974 we have seen a surge in the number of councillors who insist upon participating in management and involving themselves in ensuring that their policies are fully implemented. *Quite right too!* That is precisely what Ministers have been doing in their Whitehall Departments – and none too soon. The professional officers in local government will have to adjust positively to changes of this kind. It is not possible for them to stand in attitudes of frozen hostility or professional resentment (Widdicombe, 1986a, p. 126).

So even the Conservative secretary of state found himself in a position where he was explicitly endorsing a greater and more purposeful intervention by councillors in the way in which local authorities were run. That kind of intervention which takes different forms in different councils, has to be understood by managers and adapted to by them if they are to make an effective job of their management responsibilities.

This chapter examines the relationship between members and managers, which has been described as: 'a delicate and subtle relationship: between the lay elected Councillor and the full time professional adviser/manager' (Young, 1988 p. 1). It starts by looking at the background of councillors and how they get to be councillors; examines the different roles that they fulfil within the council – and, as important in many ways, outside the council. It will also be important to consider the extent to which practices differ very widely in different local authorities. As change is continuing to occur, the chapter also looks at the impact of politics within local government and the degree to which this is differentially affecting different councils. It will finally consider the implications of all of these changes for the management of the council as a whole, and the extent to which these changes will require a different approach and array of skills to be demonstrated by those who wish to be successful managers in local government.

Above all, it is important to stress the most significant factor for those who are senior managers in local government: with a limited number of exceptions, the elected members of an authority are directly accountable for all the actions of that council. The final decision rests with them, and that decision cannot be overridden by officials, no matter how well informed they are, how professional their judgement, or how soundly based their recommendation. As one now retired chief executive described the process to some of his senior staff: 'If it comes to a dispute between officers and members, there can only ever be one winner' (private meeting). For those who serve an elected and democratically accountable body, a recognition of that is very important, not simply for reasons of propriety and formal accountability, but also because the periodic process of election is intended to establish public acceptability of the direction the council is taking. If it were otherwise, unaccountable people could make decisions that produced broadly unpopular and unacceptable results. At an international level there is an anecdote about Lyndon Johnson which illustrates this point. As newly elected vice-president, he was desperately impressed by the team of intellectuals and executives assembled by Kennedy for his administration. He was enthusing about them to his political mentor, Sam Rayburn, Speaker of Congress. Rayburn was more cautious than Johnson, and whilst acknowledging this glittering array of talent warned him: 'I'd feel a whole lot better about them if just one of them had run for sheriff once' (Halberstam, 1973, p. 53). This anecdote, despite relating to American presidential politics, carries two powerful lessons for local government: it reflects the profound scepticism that elected members have for paid officials; and it suggests that politicians are concerned for the way in which managerial enthusiasm can lose sight of the fact that elected bodies are accountable to the people who elect them.

Who is elected?

Various official and unofficial studies of local government elected members have clearly demonstrated that neither in the past nor today are councillors representative of the population at large. Official reports carried out during the 1960s and 1970s suggested a relatively unchanged social and educational composition for the general body of councillors. More recently, studies for the Widdicombe report, and those carried out at a later date (Bloch, 1992; Kerley, 1992) have suggested that there may be some marginal but significant changes in the makeup of the membership of local authorities. However, whether then or now, in England or Scotland, a phrase that often appears to be used when discussing councillors is 'white, male, middle-aged and middle class' (Kingdom, 1991, p. 131). Research for the Widdicombe enquiry carried out in 1985 showed that, at that time, more than 80 per cent of councillors were male, 74 per cent were aged over 45, and around 70 per cent were either professionals, employers and managers or in middle-level non-manual jobs. They were – and are – likely to have left school at an older age than the majority of the population, far more likely to own their own home, far less likely to rent from a local authority, and among their number there will be more than four times as many who will have graduate or higher level qualifications than is to be found among the general population. That overall view of councillors in England, Wales and Scotland, urban and rural districts, regions and counties, does tend to disguise a far more varied pattern of membership within different councils of different types. So some councils will have no women members; in others almost half the membership will be female, with women in important positions. Younger members (if under 44 is considered young) comprise 50 per cent of the membership in the London boroughs, but less than a quarter of the membership in the regions and islands of Scotland and in the county areas of England.

This diversity has sometimes not been recognised by commentators or by government. It is arguable that the government was encouraged to established the Widdicombe enquiry on the basis of allegations made about practice of a very small number of councils. Actually this diversity of membership is matched by a considerable diversity of practice in different councils. An understanding of this is important for the manager, who should be in a position to appreciate both the particular political circumstance of the employing council and also the broader political variations found in different authorities.

The nature of the people who become councillors is influenced by a number of factors. The majority of local authorities are now dominated by representatives of political parties; there is a small –

and gradually decreasing – number of councils in which Independents form the majority of members, but these tend to be in geographically peripheral areas. It is therefore necessary in most councils for a would-be councillor to be politically active. But, it appears that, even in the most politically partisan councils, the process of recruitment of councillors is often quite fortuitous. Some current members have described just drifting into the position, others being approached by representatives of the party – in one case while standing in a cashline queue. Whilst some members will consciously set out to be selected and elected it is clear that the process of recruitment is one that is somewhat more happenstance than we would find in the selection and election of a member of parliament. Many people are elected with a generalised commitment to 'serve the community' with no very clear idea about exactly what that service will involve. Serving as a councillor is one of the few jobs in local government that does not have a job description! Indeed, one former chief executive (Barratt and Downs, 1988) attempted to carry out just this exercise for the council chairman, committee chairman, and 'backbench' members. This was prompted by the experience of being chief executive in a council with a finely balanced three-way split amongst the major parties, and a recognition that with a large number of new members it was necessary to attempt to define some agreed working practices. After protracted discussions it proved possible to agree on some.

For many members elected to serve on local authorities, with no job description and no previous experience of the activity and responsibilities they now find themselves committed to, shared agreements on patterns of working and practice are very hard to find. Newly elected members in Scotland's regions described their experience to a researcher as follows: 'They don't tell you there is no apprenticeship', 'I was not fully aware of the rules, legislation, policies, practice, budget, etc. (I could have been better informed)' (Kerley, 1992). We therefore need to recognise that on election to a local authority, councillors will not all follow the same pattern of behaviour; they will develop different different interests and apply themselves in different ways to working within the council. Being a councillor requires that the individual concerned fills one or more of a variety of roles, and does so sometimes in very individual ways, depending on the nature of the person concerned and the pattern of working in the council to which they are elected.

What do councillors do?

Numerous writers have examined the different roles of a councillor and the working practices associated with those different roles. There are, therefore, a number of different analyses which provide a helpful insight into understanding the job that councillors do and the way they do it. Heclo (1969) observed that councillors are in effect 'three men'. They are in most authorities a committee member, will be described as 'on the roads' committee by their colleagues and will often come to see the activities of the council through the perspective of one or more committees. They are also a constituency representative, and unless very confident of their political base will have to pay attention to the views of local people and generally seek to work in the interests of the local community. Councillors are also – in most cases – party activists, and therefore will be expected to represent the views of their party and seek to build support for their party.

In assessing the then current management practice and making recommendation for the management of the post-1974 local authorities, the members of the Bains Committee suggested that councillors could be defined in terms of five categories: policy-maker, welfare worker, manager, serving the community, and limiting spending. This broader variety of roles fulfilled by councillors appears quite persuasive, particular because it is given some weight by detailed examinations of politics and practice in a number of councils. One major study was carried out in pre-reorganisation Birmingham, a city where management and politics were characterised by a large and departmentalised official structure and a plethora of committees providing general political direction to that wide variety of departments and senior officials. In writing about Birmingham, Newton (1976) suggested five role-types that he found amongst councillors. He described them as follows:

- 'Parochials' appeared to be concerned exclusively with individual problems from the ward or community that they were elected for.
- 'People's agents' appear to have a wider concern for individuals – beyond simply their ward – and campaigned for 'the little person' against a large and oppressive bureaucracy, within the council and elsewhere.

- 'Policy advocates' take a broad view of policy within the council, seek to implement manifesto commitments (where there are any), and have a view across services as a whole.
- 'Policy brokers' may not be so strongly committed to particular policies as the advocates, but, as the name implies, seek to resolve differences within their party group and find a policy solution that is acceptable to most of the people involved in decision-making.
- The 'policy spokesman' will speak on behalf of constituents, but in broader terms than the parochial. The councillor here may seek to represent the class and community, a group of people with particular interests and concerns.

Most officers who have any contact with members on a continuing basis will recognise all of these role types. They may even be recognisable in terms that amount almost to caricature, as with the member whose sole concern appears to be 'my ward' and who will elevate the claimed interests of that ward over and above any other considerations that affect decision-making. This is perhaps best seen in the attitudes of some members to planning applications, or what are considered to be 'unneighbourly' facilities, such as a site for travelling people. At the other end of the continuum may be the member who appears to pay little or no regard to the ward, and focuses solely on broader council-wide issues and policies. More probably, however, in any consideration of the ways in which members of a council fulfil their role as councillors we can apply this analysis of different role types in a number of ways.

There are three significant elements to this role analysis. First, many members will demonstrate different elements of these roles in a variety of combinations. So, whilst somebody may chair the education committee, he or she may also be assiduous in pursuing individual concerns and grievances on behalf of local ward residents. Indeed, for most councillors in most authorities it is clear that regardless of their responsibilities within the council and the consequent demands upon their time the great majority of elected members take their responsibilities as a local representative very seriously. The role of representative is also seen as being important by the public, and is generally fulfilled in a satisfactory way. Research for the Widdicombe report indicated that approximately 30 per cent of the electorate could name at least one of their local councillors; in all some 20 per cent of the electorate had some kind of contact with their councillor/councillors with two-thirds of that number being satisfied with the outcome of their contact. (Widdicombe, 1986d). Some councillors, then, fulfil a number of roles, and those roles change over time. Length of service, experience and changing (probably growing) internal responsibility within the council means that many members, and particularly those with positions of responsibility, move through a continuum that starts with being a ward representative and gradually extends the demands upon them into assuming policy responsibilities. The third aspect of this analysis is that, as a group, little in the range of roles that councillors fulfil appears to have changed over time. In individual terms the leader of any council is filling his or her time very differently to how he or she did when first elected to the council. Equally, there are many councillors who are doing exactly the same things that they did ten, fifteen, or twenty years ago.

Local government managers will also need to appreciate that the manner in which councillors relate to the decision-making process and administration within the council varies substantially, both from individual to individual and between different councils. Let us consider the individual practice first. Typically, many councillors will hold 'surgeries' or 'interviews', where they make themselves available at a predetermined time and place and individual constituents or other interested parties can come and speak to them about some concern related to council business. It is a common practice, recognisable in all local authorities. It is in the follow-up to that Thursday evening or Saturday morning event that practice will vary most widely. One councillor may habitually put every concern or complaint raised to him into letter form, addressed to the appropriate chief officer. Another councillor may avoid or simply not have access to the means of generating such a complex system of correspondence. Business may be deal with by telephone and therefore may, through the nature of the medium, be more directly addressed to the responsible official within a particular department, rather than via the head of department as is more likely by letter. Yet a third member may feel that a complaint received in this way is the occasion to march in and demand an immediate interview with the appropriate director or even the chief executive of the council – perhaps first thing the next morning. Other members (and there are some, though a minority in most councils) will find that because of the nature of the community they represent there are very few complaints or concerns raised about the council, and such members often find it unnecessary to be available to electors on a regular basis. The purpose in describing this variety of practice is to illustrate the point that different councillors work in different ways, whether as ward representatives or as members of the committee, or indeed as chairman of the committee. The more general point echoes an observation made by David Walker (1993) in commenting on the position of both government ministers and councillors: 'Should we expect council leaders and committee chairs to possess managerial skills?' The position of councillors is defined by being a councillor, and the position of those who hold office in the council is defined by the office they hold – as a minimum, we can identify the committee chair by the fact that he or she sits at the top of the table. That may seem a facetious observation, but in terms of the organisation of most councils we know little more than that about what exactly is expected of somebody when they take up such a position. This is significant, because the relationship of councillors to the committees of which they are members define their activities as a councillor in many specific and often severely constraining ways.

The power of the committee

The structure of policy- and decision-making in local government is built upon a framework of committees, though their number and powers will vary from council to council. The establishment of some committees is currently mandatory for particular local authorities – for example, education committees for those councils with education responsibilities – though otherwise the form of committee structure is at the discretion of the council. In their study of councillor activities, the Audit Commission (1990) cite the example of two authorities with education responsibilities: one with a budget of £230 million per annum, which has 32 committee and subcommittee meetings per year; and the other with a budget of £160 million per annum, which has 302 committee and subcommittee meetings per year. The significance of committees in the operation of local government cannot be over-stressed: the existence of committees, their practice of working, and membership of those committees shapes and defines the way in which members see their job as a councillor. It would also appear that this may be difficult to change. The discussion on the internal management of local government which has parallelled government proposals for reorganisation has suggested that members of many councils, and commentators on council practice, find it hard to look beyond the committee model as being the appropriate way for any authority to carry out its business.

When Michael Heseltine made his major Commons statement announcing the replacement of the Community Charge or Poll Tax by the Council Tax, and his proposals for a rolling review of local government in England, he was scathing in his comments on the way in which council business was done. 'Too many members, sitting in too many meetings, making too many decisions' (Heseltine, cited in *Local Government Chronicle*, 1991). Despite some criticism of his views from many local government sources, he was not alone in his observations. Discussion with both longer serving and newly elected members suggest that many members find the time devoted to committed meetings excessive; they resent being treated as 'lobby fodder'; and for newly elected members in particular, there is also the expectation that 'as a new boy [*sic*] you just fill in the gaps' (Kerley, 1992). The research for the Widdicombe report indicated that a majority – or near majority – of councillors in all types of councils agreed that 'the present organisation of local authorities prevents them from dealing adequately with today's problems' (Widdicombe, 1986c, p. 83). Despite this concern, and despite the resentment that some members clearly feel about the demands on their time made by attendance at committee meetings, it is clear from various surveys that attendance at such meetings, preparation for them and travel to them consumes the largest amount of councillor time in all types of council. The cause of this is that the reaction of many authorities to a new challenge, or a variation of an old challenge, is to establish an appropriate committee or subcommittee to assume some kind of general oversight. The consequence is that membership of such committees becomes the most significant element of a councillor's activities.

Because the structure of committees and membership of committees is a large element of what a councillor does, much of the energy and resources of a council are put into supporting membership of such committees; and for members a vicious circle is created. They are expected to serve on committees, and carry their fair share of committee membership – in many cases they are simply expected to sit quietly and vote when asked to do so. The committee meetings are time-consuming but in an unpredictable fashion, with only the start time of the meeting printed into their diary – perhaps a year in advance. Commitment to attend such committee meetings can divert their time and energies away from the other roles they need to fill as a councillor, and many of the resources of the council are diverted into supporting such committee meetings at the expense of the other roles that a councillor is expected to fulfil. As Clarke and Stewart (1990b) observe: 'In practice councils have too often given little support to the representative roles, only giving real support to the policy and management ones' (p. 54). The practical consequence of this is that any committee or subcommittee, no matter how relatively unimportant, is given the full range of management and administrative support by the council. So, agendas will be prepared by a group of officials, there will in most councils be a pre-meeting organised for the committee or subcommittee chair, with official support from a variety of departments. The committee meeting will be attended by members and often a greater number of officials; a meticulous minute will be be taken of discussion and decisions at the meeting, and subsequently prepared for printing, circulation and retention. Many officials and members will argue that this is exactly as it should be – but at what expense? Not simply expense in terms of actual cost, but practical expense to those members in their different roles. At the same time as many councils are providing that substantial institutional support to a committee or subcommittee meeting, they are often providing next to no practical support to members in their representative role, with many members typically claiming that they must make all their own arrangements for surgeries within their wards and often do not have even minimal typing and secretarial facilities. At the broader policy level, members may have wide responsibilities outside of the council, for which again there is limited support. Typically, the leading members of any council will be expected to represent the council on local authority associations; on government working parties; and on many external bodies, including joint ventures that may have substantial financial commitments. Equally typically, those members will be sent off to such meetings unbriefed, unsupported, and rarely expected to report to their parent authority. One former councillor, now a member of parliament has described how difficult this can be for a councillor: 'A major difficulty is that we require of the member professionalism without all the tools . . . if he becomes chairman of a committee he can then begin to rely on officer support, but not normally otherwise. Once he moves beyond the local sphere, he is bereft of close support . . . if he is fortunate, he will have the help and support of officers in his own authority' (Pearman, 1990).

Just as councillors differ in the way in which they work and behave in their role as members of the council, so – as it is argued above – councils operate in different ways. Despite the institutional framework of the local government acts of 1972 and 1973 and the associated service legislation, they all work differently. Even amongst the smallest single group of comparable councils within the UK, the Scottish islands, there are different committee forms, different departmental forms, and a significant variation of status attached to respective heads of service. Among the largest and most diverse group, the English Shire districts, the differences between and among councils are legion. All such councils are, however, finding themselves subject to a variety of environmental and organisational changes that are leading to a different working relationship between councillors, within the council itself, and between councillors and officers.

A new working relationship?

Whatever the intention of the government in establishing the Widdicombe committee of enquiry into local government, the work commissioned by that committee provided a substantial body of information and understanding about the way in which members view change in local government. It also indicated some longer term changes in the way in which they view their role in the council, and the changing ways in which they work with officers.

The trends that can be observed are related, but not necessarily interrelated within individual authorities. They suggest, if anything, that some of the differences between different authorities – even among the same type of authority – are being extended and made greater, rather than that of local councils are beginning to move towards a common pattern of behaviour. The broad trends appear to suggest an increase in the number of councils which are politicised; and in councils that have been politicised for some time there appears to be a greater degree of polarisation developing. Often such change is a reaction to the attempted introduction of formalised party politics in councils where such activity did not previously exist. In councils controlled by all political parties – and in some cases by no political party – there is an increasing tendency towards a more proactive member involvement in decision-making and a shift towards a closer working relationship on policy and decision-making between members and officers. As an example, one study (Young and Davies, 1990) would suggest that between 1985 and 1989 the attendance by senior officers and chief executives at party group meetings increased in *all* types of council.

Earlier in this chapter, Young was quoted on the 'subtle' relationship between councillors and officials. He continued in his observation that that relationship worked well in a period of stable practice when there was a clear mutual understanding of the respective roles of officers and councillors. It is therefore not surprising that the period of dramatic change, and in some cases near turmoil, that has characterised the management of local government over the past fifteen to eighteen years has resulted in a recasting of that relationship between officers and members. Just as there never was a golden age when party conflict was absent from local government, so there probably never was a golden age for the relationship between councillors and senior officials. Whether we consider the relationship between chief officers as a whole and the majority group, or between an individual chief officer, senior staff in the department and the committee convener, or individual officials and individual members, then that relationship will be very different, both within and between councils. An individual councillor may seek to create a similar working relationship with different officers but not be able to do so. This may be because of the particular position and authority of the official concerned, or it may be to do with individual personality: the reasons and the circumstances will vary from time to time and in case to case. A former chief education officer described to Kogan (1974) a brusque conversation with the convener of an education sub-committee: 'He said, 'This is absurd, I am chairman of the works committee. I go along every morning at nine o'clock. I open letters and I tell the Chief Officer what replies he must make.' So I said, 'Well, you wouldn't if you were the chairman of the education committee, because I wouldn't tolerate it'. He seemed to be more astonished than annoyed and then he began to get angry' (p. 41).

If anything, it would seem that in many authorities we are seeing a movement toward a far more open and candid relationship, with a recognition that members – particularly when in a majority – will want to take an assertive view on the direction the council should take. Arun, a shire district on the Sussex coast claims to have. 'adopted a strategic management approach to its affairs since 1983. The approach has encompassed both strong political leadership and positive executive support.' One of the prime features of this is – 'policy direction by Leader and Policy Steering Group; policy implementation by chief executive and managers' (Local Government Training Board, 1988).

One of the untoward consequences of this kind of change in some councils during the 1980s was a drastic overload on the capacity of both members and senior managers to sustain and develop the activities of the organisation effectively. A wave of newer members found themselves agreeing to new policy initiatives, often involving extensive resource commitments, with an internal reshaping of the organisation, and at the same time attempting to avoid or resist government demands to reduce expenditure. The consequence was often a simple system overload, with *none* of the tasks being done very effectively. A highly self-critical report prepared by Haringey described the position in that London borough in words that could have been employed in relation to perhaps a hundred or more councils throughout the United Kingdom:

> Haringey has plenty of policies but no policy system. Haringey's policy system is characterised by drift; postponement of decisions; vagueness; excessive involvement of members and senior officers in day-to-day decisions; lack of detailed attention to implementation; lack of monitoring . . . in consequence policy vacuum (Haringey Borough Council Report, quoted in Lansley *et al.*, 1989, p. 115).

It is not surprising that during this period of turbulent change in local government we are seeing new ways of working emerging from the competing demands and pressures both within councils and from external sources. The majority of councils are seeing an increasing tendency towards members being elected at an earlier age and serving for a shorter period of time. It is precisely those members who are more likely to agree that officials have too much influence over council business, as Figure 9.1 (adapted from the Widdicombe report) indicates.

Simultaneously, there are pressures on members to change the way in which they try to assert their position within the organisation. There is an increasing tendency for leading party figures to argue that councillors should take a more strategic view of policy and decision-making in local government, and leave the detail of implementation to managers. The most senior official for the Labour Party in Scotland made this the main point of his contribution to one local government conference discussing reorganisation proposals. 'The role of councillors should be to determine the political strategy, direction and accountability of the services for which they are responsible and representing their individual local electorates . . . the Scottish Secretary of the Labour Party said' (*Scotsman*, 1993).

The nature of the changed relationship between councillors and officials, and the consequences of the various other pressures for organisational change that are occurring in local government, require us to think about both the implications for the management

FIGURE 9.1   Councillors' views on whether officials have too much influence

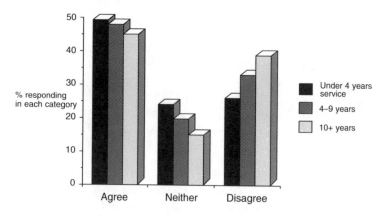

Source: D. Widdicombe (Chairman), *Research Volume II: The Local Government Councillor*, Cmnd 9798 (London: HMSO, 1986).

of the council and the skills and understanding that individual managers will have to acquire and develop.

The implications for management and managers

An increasing amount of members' time and effort in council work is being taken up by formal activities outside the committee system of the council. Councillors are expected to represent the authority on outside bodies; they are nominated to membership of school boards and governing bodies; they may have an involvement in local enterprise companies or training and enterprise councils, and perhaps extensive commitments to a similar range of bodies. In interview, one councillor formerly serving on a Scottish Region indicated that his council nominated representatives to somewhere in the region of 350 outside bodies. The process of disaggregation and fragmentation that is occurring in local government will lead to an increasing tendency for this kind of pressure on the organisation to occur in many councils. At present members who have such responsibility are often poorly served by the council. The council as a whole, and various departments within it, will need to develop more diverse management and support systems that will give members the backup they will require in taking on such responsibilities. This will also point to an increased need for councillors to have a close working relationship with a broader spread of more specialised officers within particular departments. Whilst some chief officers will still try to insist that all member contact with the department is channelled through them, the kind of changes indicated here make it less and less likely that such an arrangement will be possible – even if thought desirable, which many members clearly no longer do.

The continuing discussion on internal management in local government may not produce dramatic legislative change, but it has already in many councils led to a variety of forms of organisational experimentation. It seems improbable that we will see the total demise of the committee in local government, but the form of such committees will come to be increasingly diverse and varied. In many contracting activities the overall direction for the contracting unit is now in the hands of what in many councils has come to be called a management board, with a mixed representation of members and officials. Many authorities weight the membership of council committees to make sure that more members are on service committees than on resource and central committees. Strathclyde Region has 103 members, with 31 on the policy and resources committee, 58 on education, and 28 on each of the resource committees. It seems probable that this kind of differential commit- tee membership will not only continue to be applied in many authorities but will become more pronounced, with a far greater variety of management practice depending on the nature of the service or function involved.

When it examined the changing role of elected members, the Audit Commission entitled its report *We Can't Go On Meeting Like This* (1990). The report argued forcefully that councillors had three key roles: as 'politician', 'representative' and 'board member'. It also argued – in typically combative fashion – that members should concentrate far more of their attention on being a board member and reduce their often excessive involvement in operational manage- ment through the committee system. As is suggested above, the Audit Commission is not alone in taking this point of view and in many councils the changes that flow from this proposition are already under way. Essentially this will see members with less involvement in the detailed operational decisions of house alloca- tion, the choice between two competing tenders, or the detailed plans for a road junction improvement, and far more attention paid to setting a broad direction for the organisation. Subsequently those members will be involved in monitoring the achievement or progress towards those broad objectives, as implemented by managers within the council. The nature of such a change, where it is occurring and where it will occur, is such as to make the discussion of policy and the decisions that flow from policy far more open and more widely discussed. The consequence of this will be that such open discussion will lead to more substantial challenges to the broad strategies and policies of the council, and require a clearer and broader under- standing of what strategies and policies are arrived at. This process will in itself increasingly serve to fetter the scope that members have in the past had for ad hoc decisions relating to individual circum- stance. Related changes arising from the drive of the competitive environment will force members towards a greater concentration on a policy-making and monitoring role. This imposes a discipline on members which is not always at first apparent nor necessarily welcome. The definition of explicitly drawn policies alongside open decision-making meetings – which are now the norm after the provisions of the Freedom of Information Act (1975) – have increasingly forced members to move away from ad hoc and idiosyncratic decisions. The consequence for officials of such policy-making processes will be a requirement to operate in a more simultaneously political and professional fashion. The 'golden age myth', of members policy-making and officials administrating or implementing has always been just that – a myth. The outcome of this and related changes will oblige managers at all levels in local government to become far more sensitive to the political implications of their contribution to discussion, whether their council is party or non-party. There will be a more proactive approach to policy-making, coupled with the likelihood that implementation of that policy will be dependent on sustaining an effective network of working relationships between the variety of bodies upon which the council will depend for part of its policy programme and on which it may or may not be represented. This emerging complex of structures and relationships will require a far more sophisticated and accurate information and communication system to be employed within the council. The historical – almost caricatured – arrangement, with officers developing and presenting reports combining their preferred policy direction within terms that would be acceptable to the majority group, is unlikely to be the most effective way of securing council objectives in a new working regime. The requirement upon members, increasingly supported by and working collaboratively with officers, to go out and secure the council's objectives in collaboration with other bodies will require a far more explicit policy-led approach to decision-making. Local government managers will need to be very clear about the shape and relative influence of the network of organisational relationships within which they and the authority are going to have to work. They will also have to analyse very carefully the array of skills they are able to bring to the task of making that network of relationships work – instruction and formal procedure will not be effective in dealing with such external bodies.

Local authorities owe a duty to their managers to recognise that an ever higher proportion of their number are going to have regular working contact with elected members. In many councils, the main point of contact between members and officers has been the chief officer of a department. More recently, and particularly in the more politicised and larger authorities, members have increasingly found themselves in contact with a wider range of staff. The cadre of such staff tends to be drawn from a relatively narrow band of functions and disciplines: chief officers, deputy and assistant directors; research and committee administrative staff; some staff with area responsibilities such as planners, social services staff and housing officials. Many staff can get to a relatively senior position within the organisation with only a passing contact with elected members – and that can both limit their effectiveness within the organisation and, in the longer term, create a significant career disadvantage for them. If the various themes outlined in this chapter are accepted as pointing the general direction in which councils will increasingly come to operate, then an ever greater proportion of those staff are going to need an understanding and experience of that close working relationship with more and more councillors. That will require a change in attitude on the part of many of the people involved – on both sides – and a requirement for positive support and training on both sides in the process (officers and members). Kogan (1974) draws attention to the former chief education officer of Leeds admitting his weakness in not understanding the political perspective within the majority group on a major development project that he had under discussion with central government, which had secured substantial central government funding. 'Party policy in many Labour controlled councils was decided by "the group". I had no contact with the group, of course, being an officer, and the project was turned down' (p. 42). This extract is revealing in two senses. The least important is that twenty or more years ago even such a senior official had no formal contact with the majority group – a position that simply would not obtain now in most councils. Second, and perhaps more importantly, it reveals the remarkable political naivety of somebody who had managed to achieve senior office within his profession and within local government. Such naivety can still be found, and it would still represent a significant handicap to any senior manager in local government. Among the managers concerned and the councils in which they work we have to find ways of ensuring that such behaviour is a phenomenon of the past.

It has been argued in this chapter that the relative balance between members and mangers is changing, but changing in many different ways in different councils. There is no clear pattern to that change, but it does give a clear indication of the degree of turbulence which is to be found in the operation of local government. Young was quoted earlier as referring to the 'delicate and subtle relationship' that exists between members and officials. That relationship is undoubtedly being reshaped in many councils, and will have to be in many others. The way in which it is being reshaped gives an indication of the overall direction and future of management change that we may see in local government.

Some points for discussion

1. What is the new role for members in a changing pattern of local government?
2. How should members manage?
3. Should the role of the councillor be made more professional – like members of Parliament?
4. Do members have the necessary support, skills and training to do an effective job?

10 The Future Management of Local Government

It clear that there will continue to be great deal of uncertainty about the future of local government. In England the Local Government Commission carries on with its rolling programme of review, with the one sure consequence of creating enmity and souring future necessary working relationships at every stopping point. In Wales and Scotland the government has not yet completed the necessary legislative programme to reorganise local government, and the plans continue to be highly controversial. The turbulence in both the environmental framework within which local government works (does it have any responsibilities for post-school education?) and the manner in which councils are expected to work (must all activities be put onto a contractual or quasi- contractual basis – and with whom?) is of a degree which members and officials of even ten years ago would not recognise.

The economic climate suggests that for the foreseeable future there will continue to be considerable pressure on local authorities to restrain expenditure and seek alternative means of securing growth in services where it is thought appropriate. It would appear that the newly created authorities will be very receptive to that message. The form of organisation that the new councils create will emphasise a wish to secure the most effective delivery to the consumer of council services and management structures are being shaped accordingly. All of this suggests that the emphasis on sharpening the management of local government will continue, with all the implications that will have for the local government manager. This final chapter considers the likely prospects for future change in local government in Great Britain, considers the implications for the management of local government and the likely consequences for the working practice and careers of local government managers.

The future of local government

The past behaviour of central government over many years would suggest that it recognises a need for local government, in order to deliver many of the goods and services which characterise a developed industrial society. After the knockdown and drag-out battles of the 1980s (in which local government got most of the knocking down) there seem to be signs of a more emollient attitude on the part of some ministers. It does still seem to be the case – under both major parties – that central government has some difficulties with the idea of local democracy. In effect, governments of all kinds like their own view to prevail, and see local government not as an expression of self-government for a community, but a subordinate institution best equipped to follow encouragement and direction, failing which instruction and coercion will be necessary. This view may suggest that, whilst the form of local government may remain, there is an increasing likelihood that the discretion and choice generally thought to be an inherent characteristic of freely elected institutions will increasingly be curtailed. Services will be defined on a contractual basis; the extent and scope of some activities defined more prescriptively by central government, or central government agencies. This may be a trend which will lead to a far more regimented and predictable form of local government – in effect, a form of local administration.

Alternatively, we can recognise that some sense of locality is important to our civic culture and people value it, even if it is John Major nostalgically recalling Middlesex County as he watches cricket at their ground. Such an expression is not mere nostalgia, but is given clear recognition in the research studies of the Widdicombe Committee. Those studies (Widdicombe, 1986d) show that a large proportion of the people surveyed thought that local government runs things 'well or fairly well'. More important in this context is the very strong public support for the continued *election* of local government. Almost 80 per cent of those who were surveyed thought it would be a bad idea – and 56 per cent thought it 'very bad' – if members of local government were appointed by central government. A somewhat more sophisticated view is indicated of the contribution that elected representatives make than might sometimes appear to be the case. Over 60 per cent of the survey group think their local council should try to do 'its best for the area', whereas approximately half that number think that should be the role of the member of parliament.

There may well therefore be limited popular support for the continuing government programme of shifting powers and responsibilities to appointed – or even self-appointed – local bodies such as health boards and training and enterprise or local enterprise companies. The test for the public acceptability of such organisational arrangements will be the degree to which they can be, or are willing to be, publicly accountable. In this, of course, such bodies start from a poor base; to that extent elected local government has a strong appeal to the large majority of the population who place a considerable value on such public accountability. Making a virtue and a strength of that particular quality of public accountability characteristic of elected local government will be the major strategic challenge for local government in the next few years.

The management of local government in the 1990s

In a number of different ways, the transition that local government is going through is not dissimilar to the changes that are occurring in Eastern Europe. There is a transition from the former model of a command economy, where decisions made in the centre (the council or committee) would be implemented by subordinate bodies (officials) through a vertically integrated structure (the directly employed workforce) on a programmatic basis (we paint these houses this year; those next), to grateful recipients with limited choice. In addition, there are few if any price signals within the system of decision-making, because few of the activities of the organisation are priced, and volume control is the general practice. This may be a caricature, but caricature is intended to make a point by exaggeration, and in such circumstances exaggeration is both necessary and permitted. The management of the uncertainty caused by the change from such a regime to one that is far removed from it is demanding and unsettling for all those involved – members, senior managers and staff – but it is inevitable and it is necessary. That adjustment of practice and attitude will take several different forms:

- Councils will have to adjust to the expectation that they can no longer instruct and expect obedience. Alexander and Orr (1994) have demonstrated the extent to which councils of all types, whether in areas of multiple urban stress or rural tranquillity, are now increasingly dependent upon a network of working relationships for the development and implementation of their ambitions. Initiating and progressing change through this network will require a very different range of management and information systems to those in place within many councils. It will also require a change of attitude among councillors and council leaders. The assumption that the council and its committees are at the centre of the known universe will come under increasing pressure. If councils are increasingly reliant upon sustaining this policy network, then they will have drastically to improve the level of support and assistance that is provided to those who represent them within that network. As was argued in the previous chapter, such support outside the confines of the council is poor or even nonexistent for councillors, and little better for officials, in most councils. Not only that, but it is perhaps poor because it is not yet recognised as being important. Strathclyde Region is the largest council in Britain, with a budget of £2 thousand million, and tied into a policy network of organisations outside the council with a total budget of perhaps double that. In 1990 the membership of the council of 103 members was split between four parties, with Labour holding approximately 90 of the seats. Despite this overwhelming voting dominance, Labour members were reminded officially by group officers that their first priority as councillors was to attend committee meetings, even if it meant missing the board meeting of a company or other agency on which they represented the region, and where they might be party to critical decisions.

- Councils will have to create information systems which will enable them to scan their working environment effectively; in effect to keep an eye on the various organisations the council must relate to and which relate to the members of the communities which the council serves and represents. Large bureaucracies are often ill-equipped to look outside the organisation, either for information or example – they will need to develop or acquire the capacity to do so. They will also need to recognise that, just as military forces throughout history have relied on irregular scouts to provide them with advance information, so councils will come to rely on irregulars to do just that. At the time of writing, Stevenage Council is advertising for an official to be responsible for 'Local monitoring and Community Development' (*Guardian*, 1993). They explain: 'Local services such as health education and employment services are becoming less accountable to the communities they serve. The Council is intent on counteracting this trend and has set up a new committee to monitor local services . . . the person appointed will develop wide ranging contacts with other bodies, undertake research and maintain information on local services.' Such monitoring will aid the council in understanding what is happening in these other agencies, and help it in the representative role that the council must take on to maintain some accountability to the public – albeit surrogate accountability – for these still *public* services.

- Councils are also having to put considerable energies and investment into managing the policy network within the organisation itself. It is rare today for a new challenge to be of a type that is comfortably handled within the confines of one department or one committee. The alternative and historically popular recourse of setting up another committee is discouraged in many councils, for reasons of cost and maintaining corporate cohesion. So the organisational dilemma is often to find ways of tackling multifunctional issues in a coordinated way. Maintaining organisational cohesion and integration has always been a dilemma for complex organisations in a turbulent and rapidly changing environment. As Lawrence and Lorsch (1967) in their classic study of organisational form in different working environments also point out, it is costly. Companies operating in such an environment incur management costs perhaps more than 20 per cent greater than those with a more stable and predictable working environment. Yet councils are increasingly going to be forced to develop effective systems and processes to address new concerns relating to the local physical environment, public health and social policy changes, and economic restructuring.

- It will also become more necessary for local authorities to develop clear and explicit policy strategies for their various interests and service programmes. This may well seem to contradict the scepticism expressed earlier in this book about the processes of rational planning lauded by some management theorists and practitioners, and most effectively debunked by the enthusiasts of the 'excellence' school of management, but it seems important to stress a subtle difference here. Effective planning and strategy development may prove to be messy and iterative in form, rather than the neatly wrapped and tied process that has been implied in the past. Nonetheless, such planning has to start somewhere, particularly if it is to be the subject of complex and articulated negotiation with a variety of other potential beneficiaries of and stakeholders in the policy process. Such negotiation implies flexibility as to means, but requires clarity of intended outcomes – admittedly a state of perfection that many of us aspire to but few achieve. Local authorities tend, on the whole, to have long-standing and skilled practice at developing formalised and often inflexible procedures and systems, but have less confidence in clearly expressing intended outcomes.

- Consider one example of this weakness. In May 1993, Calderdale Council were reported on the Radio 4 *Today Programme* as being in the process of considering attaching electronic tags to elderly residents in their old folks' homes. This was in response to a couple of occasions when confused residents had taken a late-night wander out of the building. The report was introduced by an angry condemnation of the idea by the local MP, as yet another example of underfunding, understaffing and cuts in social work services. The idea was potentially controversial, and had implications for civil liberties and individual preferences yet – since many hospitals now similarly tag newborn babies – it also had some positive aspects. When interviewed, the chair of the social services committee was not able to make clear what the intention of the council was, and when asked whether the residents had been asked, responded with the deathless – 'Not yet, because it hasn't been to committee'.

- Just as it is suggested that councils will have to develop new ways of exercising their duties as the only elected representative body for the community, so it will also be necessary to assess effectively their internal capacity for acknowledging the demands of the individual as a consumer of council services. The impetus of the Citizen's Charter and other related social changes discussed earlier in the book will put considerable pressure on councils to review how the effectiveness of their implementation of the canon of consumer rights and principles. A decline in collective organisation is often matched by an increased assertiveness at an individual level – as can be seen already in the growing tendency of individuals to pursue claims to an industrial tribunal or ombudsman. Individuals, whether as the consumers of council services, employees, or residents, are increasingly likely to challenge the decisions and actions of the council. Whether Halford in the case of Merseyside alleging gender discrimination, or a group of families in Orkney claiming poor and ill-judged professional practice, getting it wrong can be very expensive for the authority, whether in time, energy, money and reputation.

Because of the factors indicated here, and the many other reasons discussed elsewhere in this book, there seems every indication that local authorities are going to have to continue to sharpen up their management practice. They will also need to continue to press their senior staff to be more effective managers, so we now turn to the characteristics and experience which the effective manager of the future will have to demonstrate.

The future manager in local government

This concluding section is not intended to be a series of career hints. It does however reflect one assessment of what expectations the local authorities of the future will have of their managers. It could therefore be taken to imply what qualities they will seek in those they consider appointing, and what experience and achievement they will look for in those whom they do appoint:

- For many and complex reasons local government is unlikely to abandon the professional (in the broadest sense) entry point to a career in a particular function, or in local government generally. Essentially this is because local government does things which it cannot readily diversify away from, and therefore it needs people to do them as effectively as they can. It is likely, however, that the successful senior managers in local government will in the future be those who are ready to extend the scope of their understanding and activities beyond the boundaries of their base profession. It may challenge a traditional sense of value and comfort, but doing the same job well – even very well – for a long time will have to be its own reward, for it is unlikely to be rewarded by career advancement.

- In a more intensely political environment the good manager will be the one who has developed a good measure of political sensitivity. This does not imply party membership or even sympathy, but the demonstration of an awareness that members have a political agenda and seek an understanding of that. In the best of councils that will increasingly mean an understanding that enables the manager to debate and challenge that agenda, testing its capacity for effective implementation.

- The effective manager will increasingly be aware of the extent to which the council is not the sole provider of public services, and all of the implications that has for policy and management practice. There may be formal competition, or it may be overt and informal, but service delivery in many of the council's activities will increasingly be tested against alternative benchmarks. It will be tested by ever more discriminating and assertive consumers, who will come to expect services to meet their requirements and to be shaped to *their* pattern of convenience and expectation rather than that of the council and its employees. Even our vocabulary will have to change; not in the fine definition discussed in Chapter 8, but in abandoning the casual references to the public as 'the punters', 'Joe public', or 'the great unwashed' (all heard in council offices; used by council officers).

- Just as some consumers are more assertive, so there are many who are just not assertive enough. Many groups in society get a raw deal from their local council or councils, and as we become more aware of this so it seem less acceptable – and less socially desirable. Minority ethnic communities, women and physical communities are often the subjects of – rarely now intentional but nonetheless real – discrimination. Whilst the Citizen's Charter lauded equal opportunities as a key principle of public service, the first report on progress omitted that aspect of achievement (Cabinet Office, 1993). It is unlikely that the new local authorities will be so casual, and they will expect managers to be more sensitive to the equal opportunities aspects of both policy development and implementation.

Conclusion

The reorganisation of local government will introduce many changes and a new shape to local government throughout the mainland of the UK. It will also see job losses, and it is certain that the new authorities will not staff themselves in the way they did some twenty years ago. The need for effective management will be even greater than it was in the past, as will be the need for effective managers.

This book opened with a phrase from Alexander Hamilton. It may be an extravagant comparison, but a former leader of Lewisham council made very similar comments to his local Labour Party some two hundred years later. It seems an appropriate comment on which to close a book on managing in local government:

> The issue of management has nothing to do with ideology or philosophy. All ideologies and philosophies have to be implemented in an effective way . . . we must urgently begin the process of transforming this authority into one that truly serves the interests of working people by using efficiently and effectively the large sums of money we take from their pockets (Sullivan, quoted in Lansley *et al.*, 1989, p. 116).

Bibliography

Alexander, A. (1982a) *The Politics of Local Government in the United Kingdom* (London: Longman).

Alexander, A. (1982b) *Local Government in Britain since Reorganisation* (London: Allen & Unwin).

Alexander, A. (1992) *Things Fall Apart? – Some Thoughts on the Fragmentation of the Local Public Sector'*, Local Government Studies, vol. 16, no. 1, pp. 9–13.

Alexander, A., and Orr K. (1994) *Managing the Fragmented Authority* (Luton: Local Government Management Board).

Allison, G. T. (1983) 'Public and Private Management: Are They Fundamentally Alike in All Unimportant Respects?', in J. L. Perry and K. L. Kraemer (eds), *Public Management: Public and Private Perspectives* (California: Mayfield)

Arnold, J., Hope, T, and Southworth, A. (1985) *Financial Accounting* (London: Prentice-Hall).

Ascher, K. (1987) *The Politics of Privatisation* (London: Macmillan).

Audit Commission (1986) *Performance Review: A Handbook* (London: HMSO).

Audit Commission (1988a) *The Competitive Council* (London: HMSO).

Audit Commission (1988b) *Better Financial Management* (London: HMSO).

Audit Commission (1989a) *Better Financial Management*, Management Paper No. 3 (London: HMSO).

Audit Commission (1989b) *Managing Services Effectively: Performance Review*, Management Paper No. 5 (London: HMSO).

Audit Commission (1990) *We Can't Go On Meeting Like This: The Changing Role of Local Authority Members*, Management Paper No. 8 (London: HMSO).

Audit Commission (1991) *People Management: Human Resources in Tomorrow's Public Services*, Management Paper No. 9 (London: HMSO).

Audit Commission (1992a) *The Citizen's Charter: Performance Indicators* (London: Audit Commission).

Audit Commission (1992b) *The Publication of Information (Standards of Performance) Direction 1992* (London: Audit Commission).

Audit Commission (1993) *Realising the Benefits of Competition: The Client Role for Contracted Services* (London: HMSO).

Bains, M. (Chairman) (1972) *The New Local Authorities: Management and Structure* (London: HMSO).

Barratt, J. and Downs, J. (1988) *Organising for Local Government: A Local Political Responsibility* (London: Longman).

Bedfordshire County Council (1991) *Job Description for Chief Executive*.

Beishon, J. (1989) 'Empowering Consumers', *New Socialist*, June–July 1989, pp. 16–17.

Benham, H. (1964) *Two Cheers for the Town Hall* (London: Hutchinson).

Berkshire County Council (1992) *Management Budget 1992/93* (Reading: The County Council).

Bichard, M. (1991) *Interview on Today Programme*, Radio 4, 9 April.

Bleasdale, A. (1993) *On the Ledge* (unpublished).

Bloch, A. (1992) *The Turnover of Local Authority Councillors* (London: Policy Studies Institute).

Blunkett, D. and Green, G. (1983) *Building from the Bottom: The Sheffield Experience*, Tract 491 (London: Fabian Society).

Blunkett, D. and Jackson, K. (1987) *Democracy in Crisis: The Town Halls Respond* (London: Hogarth Press).

Braine, J. (1989) *Room at the Top* (London: Mandarin).

Bramley, G. (1990) 'The Demand for Local Government Services – Survey Evidence on Usage, Distribution and Externalities', *Local Government Studies*, November/December 1990.

Brand, J. (1974) *Local Government Reform in England* (London: Croom Helm).

Brooke, R. (1989) *Managing the Enabling Authority* (London: Longman).

Byrne, T. (1986) *Local Government in Britain* (Harmondsworth: Penguin).

Cabinet Office Efficiency Unit (1991) *Making the Most of Next Steps: The Management of Ministers' Departments and Their*

Executive Agencies, Report to the Prime Minister (London: HMSO).

Cabinet Office (1993) *Citizen's Charter – Report on the First Year* (London: HMSO).

Cambridgeshire County Council (1990) *Performance Management* (Cambridge: The County Council).

Carter, N., Klein, R. and Day, P. (1991) *How Organisations Measure Success* (London: Routledge).

Castle, B. (1980) *The Castle Diaries 1974–76* (London: Weidenfeld & Nicolson).

Caulfield, I., and Schultz, J. (1989) *Planning for Change: Strategic Planning in Local Government* (Harlow: Longman).

Central Statistical Office (1993) *United Kingdom National Accounts* (London: HMSO).

CIPFA Scottish Branch (1990) *Local Government Finance in Scotland: A Handbook* (Edinburgh: CIPFA).

Clarke, M., and Stewart, J. (1985) *Local Government and the Public Service Orientation* (Luton: LGTB).

Clarke, M. and Stewart, J. (1986a) *The Public Service Orientation: Issues and Dilemmas To Be Faced* (Luton: LGTB).

Clarke, M. and Stewart, J. (1986b) *The Public Service Orientation – Developing the Approach* (Luton: LGTB).

Clarke, M., and Stewart, J. (1988) *The Enabling Council* (Luton: LGTB).

Clarke, M., and Stewart, J. (1990) *Developing Effective Public Service Management* (Luton: LGTB).

Clarke, M., and Stewart, J. (1990a) *General Management in Local Government: Getting the Balance Right* (Harlow: Longman).

Commission for Local Authority Accounts in Scotland (1992) *Consultation Paper: Performance Indicators* (Edinburgh: CLAAS).

Commission for Local Authority Accounts in Scotland (1992) *The Publication of Information (Standards of Performance) Direction 1992* (Edinburgh: CLAAS).

Crossman, R. H. S. (1975) *Diaries of a Cabinet Minister, vol. I* (London: Hamish Hamilton).

Croydon, London Borough of (1992) *Annual Report and Accounts 1991/92* (London: The Council).

Davies, H. (1987) 'Local Government Under Siege', Speech to the Annual Conference of the Society of Local Authority Chief Executives, Nottingham, 8 July.

Davies, H. (1992) *Fighting Leviathan: Building Social Markets that Work* (London: Social Market Foundation).

Davies, J. (1972) *The Evangelistic Bureaucrat* (London: Tavistock).

Deal, T. E., and Kennedy, A. A. (1982) *Corporate Culture* (Reading, Mass: Addison-Wesley).

Dearlove, J. (1973) *The Politics of Policy in Local Government* (Cambridge: University Press).

Dearlove, J. (1979) *The Reorganisation of British Local Government* (Cambridge: University Press).

Deloitte Haskins and Sells/IFF Research Ltd (1989) *Training in Britain: Employers' Activities* (London: HMSO).

Department of the Environment (1983) *Streamlining the Cities*, Cmnd 9005 (London: HMSO).

Department of the Environment (1991a) *The Internal Management of Local Authorities in England: A Consultation Paper* (London: HMSO).

Department of the Environment (1991b) *The Structure of Local Government in England: A Consultation Paper* (London: HMSO).

Donoghue, B., and Jones G. W. (1973) *Herbert Morrison: Portrait of a Politician* (London: Weidenfeld & Nicolson).

Dopson, S. and Stewart, R. (1988) *The Changing Functions of Lower and Middle Management* (Oxford: Templeton College Working Paper).

Dopson, S., and Stewart, R. (1989a) *Widening the Debate on Public and Private Sector Management* (Oxford: Templeton College Working Paper).

Dopson, S., and Stewart, R. (1989b) *What Is Happening to Middle Management?* (Oxford: Templeton College Working Paper).

Drucker, P. (1954) *Principles of Management* (London: Heinemann).

Drucker, P. (1968) *The Practice of Management* (London: Pan).

Drucker, P. (1974) *Management: Tasks, Responsibilities, Practices* (London: Heinemann).

Dunleavy, P. (1980) *Urban Political Analysis* (London: Macmillan).

Dunleavy, P. (1984) 'The Limits to Local Government', in M. Boddy and C. Fudge (eds), *Local Socialism?* (London: Macmillan).

Dunleavy, P. (1986) 'Explaining the Privatisation Boom', *Public Administration*, vol. 61, pp. 13–34.

Dunsire, A. (1973) *Administration: The Word and the Science* (London: Martin Robertson).

Durham County Council (1991) *Annual Report 1990/91* (Durham: The Council).

Dykes, H (1990) Interview in *Left, Right and Centre*, BBC1 Scotland, 2 March.

Ealing, London Borough of (n.d.–1992?) *Closer to Excellence – A Management Development Strategy for Ealing* (London: The Council).

Ealing, London Borough of (1991) *Business Planning Progress Report* (London: The Council).

Economist, The (1991) 'John Major's Charter', 27 July.

Edinburgh District Council (1993) *General Services Survey 1992* (Edinburgh: The Council).

Elcock, H. J. (1986) *Local Government: Politicians, Professionals and the Public, in Local Authorities* (London: Methuen).

Elcock, H., and Jordan, A. G. (eds) (1987) *Learning from Local Authority Budgeting* (Aldershot: Avebury Press).

Elcock, H., Jordan A. G., and Midwinter, A. F. (1989) *Budgeting in Local Government: Managing the Margins* (London: Longman).

Flynn, N. (1990) *Public Sector Management* (Brighton: Harvester Wheatsheaf).

Flynn, N., and Walsh, K. (1987) *Competitive Tendering* (University of Birmingham: Institute of Local Government Studies).

Forsyth, M. (1980) *Re-servicing Britain* (London: Adam Smith Institute).

Foster, J. (1992) 'People Recognised as Key to Profitability', *Scotsman*, 24 January, p. 29.

Fowler, M. (1975) *Personnel Management in Local Government* (London: IPM).

Fowler, M. (1988) *Human Resource Management in Local Government* (Harlow: Longman).

Fraser, D (1979) *Power and Authority in the Victorian City* (Oxford: Basil Blackwell).

Frater, M. (1992) *Kent County Council – A Case Study* (Maidstone: Kent County Council).

Fulton, Lord, (Chairman) (1968) *The Civil Service: Report of a Committee of Enquiry*, Cmnd 3638 (London: HMSO).

Game, C. (1987) 'Birmingham City Council' in H. Elcock, and A. G. Jordan (eds) *Learning from Local Authority Budgeting* (Aldershot: Avebury Press).

Gilbert, J. (1992) 'Step Up', *Social Work Today*, 23 January, pp. 27–30.

Gloucestershire County Council (1989) *Code of Practice for Personnel Management* (Gloucester: The County Council).

Goss, S. (1989) *Local Labour and Local Government* (Edinburgh: University Press).

Green, D. (1981) *Power and Party in an English City* (London: Allen & Unwin).

Guardian (1992) Society pages advertisements, Wednesdays, 5 February to 25 March.

Guardian (1993) Society pages advertisements, Wednesday 19 May.

Gunn, L. (1987) 'Perspectives on Public Management' in J. Kooiaman and K. A. Eliasson (eds), *Managing Public Organisations: Lessons from Contemporary European Experience* (London: Sage).

Gunn, L. (1992) 'The Effective Manager in Local Government' (Glasgow: mimeo).

Gyford, J. (1984) *Local Politics in Britain*, 2nd edn (London: Croom Helm).

Gyford, J. (1991) *Citizens, Consumers and Councils* (London: Macmillan).

Gyford, J., Leach S., and Game, C. (1989) *The Changing Politics of Local Government* (London: Unwin Hyman).

Halberstam, D. (1973) *The Best and the Brightest* (London: Pan).

Hampton, W. (1970) *Democracy and Community* (Oxford University Press).

Hampton, W. (1987) *Local Government and Urban Politics* (London: Longman).

Handy, C., Gordon, C., Gow, I., and Randlesome, C. (1988) *Making Managers* (London: Pitman).

Heclo, H., and Wildavsky, A. (1974) *The Private Government of Public Money* (London: Macmillan).

Heclo, H. (1969) 'The Councillors Job', *Public Administration*, vol. 47, no. 1.

Hegarty, S. (1992) 'An Entrepreneur at the Council', *Independent*, 4 June, p. 24.

Henney, A. (1984) *Inside Local Government: A Case for Radical Reform* (London: Sinclair Browne).

HM Government (1980) *Local Government Planning and Land Act 1980* (London: HMSO).

HM Government (1981) *Alternatives to Domestic Rates*, Cmnd 8499 (London: HMSO).

HM Government (1985) *Competition in the Provision of Local Authority Services – A Consultation Paper* (London: HMSO).

HM Government (1985) *Financial Management in Government Departments*, Cmnd 9058 (London: HMSO).

HM Government (1986) *Paying for Local Government*, Cmnd 9714 (London: HMSO).

HM Government (1988) *Local Government Act 1980* (London: HMSO).

HM Government (1989) *Training in Britain – The Main Report* (London: HMSO).

HM Government (1989) *Caring for People*, Cmnd 849 (London: HMSO).

HM Government (1990a) *A Guide for New Managers* (London: HMSO).

HM Government (1990b) *Measuring Up: Performance Indicators in Further Education* (London: HMSO).

HM Government (1991a) *The Citizen's Charter*, Cmnd 1599 (London: HMSO).

HM Government (1991b) *Competing for Quality: Purchasing Public Services*, Cmnd 1730 (London: HMSO).

HM Government (1991c) *Competing for Quality: Competition in the Provision of Local Services – A Consultation Paper* (London: HMSO).

Heseltine, M. (1980) 'Ministers and Management in Whitehall', *Management Services in Government*, no. 35.

Hill, L. A. (1991) *Becoming a Manager* (Cambridge, Mass: Harvard University Press).

Hood, C. (1983) *The Tools of Government* (Oxford: Martin Robertson).

Hood, C. (1990) *Beyond the Public Bureaucracy State? Public Administration in the 1990s* (London: LSE).

Hood, C. (1991) 'A Public Management for All Seasons', *Public Administration*, vol. 69, Spring, pp. 3–17.

House of Commons (1991) *Next Steps Agencies: Third Report of the Home Affairs Committee*, Paper 177 (London: HMSO).

House of Commons (1993) *Treasury and Civil Service Committee: Responsibilities and Work of the Office of Public Service and Science*, Paper 390-i (London: HMSO).

Hughes, C. (1992) 'A Revolution That Will Go On', *Independent*, 2 April.

Industrial Relations Review and Report (1992) 525, December (London: Industrial Relations Services).

INLOGOV (1989) *Report on the Organisation and Management of the Education Department, Strathclyde Regional Council* (Birmingham: INLOGOV).

Jones, G. W., and Stewart, J. (1983) *The Case for Local Government* (London: Allen & Unwin).

Jones, J. H. (1992) *Troubleshooter 2* (London: BBC Books).

Joint Local Authority Associations (1983) *Rate Support Grant* (London: mimeo).

Johnston, T. (1952) *Memories* (Glasgow: Collins).

Keating, M., and Boyle, R. (1986) *Re-making Urban Scotland* (Edinburgh University Press).

Kanter, R. M. (1990) *The Change Masters* (London: Unwin).

Keating, M., and Midwinter, A. (1983) *The Government of Scotland* (Edinburgh: Mainstream).

Kerley, R., and Wynn, D. (1991) 'Competitive Tendering: The Transition to Contracted Services in Scottish Local Authorities', *Local Government Studies*, vol. 17, no. 5, pp. 33–52.

Kerley, R. (1989) *Training for Staff Involved in Economic Development in Local Government* (Edinburgh: Convention of Scottish Local Authorities/Scottish Local Authorities Management Centre).

Kerley, R. (1992) *Changing the Guard* (Glasgow: Scottish Local Authorities Management Centre and Joseph Rowntree Foundation).

Kerley, R. (1993a) 'Retiral and Replacement of Elected Members in the Scottish District Elections of 1992' (Glasgow: Scottish Local Authorities Management Centre, mimeo).

Kerley, R. (1993b) *Equal Opportunities in Practice* (Glasgow: Scottish Local Authorities Management Centre, mimeo).

Kerley, R. (1993c) 'Management Appraisal in Practice', *Public Administration*, winter.

Kerley, R. (1993d) 'Survey of Participants – The Manager in Local Government Course 1989–92' (Glasgow: Scottish Local Authorities Management Centre, mimeo).

Kingdom, J. (1991) *Local Government and Politics in Britain* (Hemel Hempstead: Philip Allan).

Kirklees Metropolitan Council (1991) *Our Vision for Kirklees* (Huddersfield: The Council).

Kline, J., and Malaber, J. (1986) *Whose Value? Whose Money?* (London: Local Government Information Unit).

Knight, B. (1983) *Managing School Finance* (London: Heinemann).

Kogan, M. (1974) *County Hall* (Harmondsworth: Penguin).

Labour Coordinating Committee (1989) *Public Management for New Times* (London: LCC).

Labour Party (1991) *Citizen's Charter: Labour's Better Deal for Consumers and Citizens* (London: Labour Party).

Laffin, M. (1986) *Professionalism and Policy: The Role of the Professions in the Central–Local Relationship* (Aldershot: Gower).

Laffin, M. (1989) *Managing under Pressure* (London: Macmillan).

Laffin, M., and Young, K. (1985) 'The Changing Roles and Responsibilities of Local Authority Chief Officers', *Public Administration*, vol. 63, pp. 41–59.

Lansley, S., Goss, S., and Wolmar, C. (1989) *Councils in Conflict* (London: Macmillan).

Lawrence, P. R., and Lorsch, J. (1967) *Organisation and Environment* (Cambridge, Mass: Harvard University Press).

Leicester District Council (n.d.) *City Council Charter* (Leicester: The Council).

Liberal Democratic Party (1991) *Citizens' Britain – Liberal Democrat Policies for a People's Charter* (London: Liberal Democrats).

Local Authority Accounts Commission for Scotland (1992) 'Consultation Paper: Performance Indicators' (Edinburgh: mimeo).

Local Government Chronicle (1990) 'News Report', 31 May.

Local Government Chronicle (1991) 'Local Government Reform', 14 June.

Local Government Information Unit (1993) *The LGIU Guide to Local Government Finance* (London: LGIU).

Local Government Management Board (1990) *Achieving Success: a Corporate Training Strategy* (Luton: LGMB).

Local Government Management Board (1992) *Competences*, vol. 1, no. 1 (Luton: LGMB).

Local Government Management Board (1993) *The Well Managed Authority* (Luton: LGMB).

Local Government Training Board (1985) *The Management Challenge for Local Government* (Luton: LGTB).

Local Government Training Board (1987) *Getting Closer to the Public* (Luton: LGTB).

Local Government Training Board (1988) *Going for Better Management* (Luton: LGTB).

Lothian Regional Council (1992) *Report and Accounts, 1991–92* (Edinburgh: Lothian Region).

Lothian Regional Council (1993) *Employee Development Services 1993/94* (Edinburgh: Lothian Region).

Loughlin, M. (1986) *Local Government in the Modern State* (London: Sweet & Maxwell).

Loughlin, M., Gelfand M., and Young K. (1985) *Half a Century of Municipal Decline 1935–1985* (London: Allen & Unwin).

Lucey, T. (1985) *Management Accounting* (Eastleigh: DP Publications).

Mallaby, Sir G. (Chairman) (1967) *Committee on the Staffing of Local Government*, Report (London: HMSO).

Maud, Sir John (Chairman) (1967) *Committee on the Management of Local Government, Vol. 1*, Report (London: HMSO).

Metcalfe, L., and Richards, S. (1990) *Improving Public Management* (London: Sage).

Midwinter, A. (1984) *The Politics of Local Spending* (Edinburgh: Mainstream).

Midwinter, A., and Mair, C. (1987) *Rates Reform* (Edinburgh: Mainstream).

Midwinter, A., Keating, M., and Mitchell, J. (1991) *Politics and Public Policy in Scotland* (London: Macmillan).

Mintzberg, H. (1980) *The Nature of Managerial Work* (New York: Harper and Row).

Mori (1991) *Survey for the National Consumer Council* (London NCC).

Nairn District Council (1992) *Annual Report and Accounts 1991/92* (Nairn: The Council).

National Consumer Council (1986) *Measuring Up: Consumer Assessment of Local Authority Services* (London: NCC).

National Consumer Council and Mori (1991) *Consumer Concerns 1991: A Consumer View of Public and Local Authority Services* (London: NCC).

National Training Awards (1993) *Winners 1992 – Annual Report* (Sheffield: Employment Department Group).

Newton, K. (1976) *Second City Politics* (Oxford: University Press).

Newton, K., and Karran, T. (1985) *The Politics of Local Expenditure* (London: Macmillan).

Niskanen, W. (1971) *Bureaucracy and Representative Government* (New York: Aldine-Atherton).

Open University (1993) *Public Services and the Consumer*, Audio Tape for Course B887: Managing Public Services.

Organisation for Economic Cooperation and Development (1989) *Survey of Public Management Developments 1988* (Paris: OECD).

PA/*Local Government Chronicle* (1990) *Management of Change* (London: PA).

Paterson, I. (Chairman) (1973) *The New Scottish Local Authorities: Organisation and Management Structures* (Edinburgh: Scottish Development Department).

Pearman, J. (1990) 'The Professionalisation of the Elected Member', *Education*, June.

Perry, J. L. and Kraemer, K. L. (1983) *Public Management: Public and Private Perspectives* (California: Mayfield).

Peters, T. (1989) *Thriving on Chaos* (London: Pan).

Peters, T., and Waterman, R. (1982) *In Search of Excellence* (London: Harper & Row).

Pollitt, C. J. (1986) 'Beyond the Managerial Model: The Case for Broadening Performance Assessment in Government and the Public Services', *Financial Accountability and Management*, vol. 2, no. 3, pp. 155–170.

Pollitt, C. J. (1990) *Managerialism and the Public Services: the Anglo–American Experience* (Oxford: Basil Blackwell).

Prowle, M., and Hines, G. (1989) *Local Government Competition: Meeting the Challenge* (London: ACCA).

Public Administration (1991) Themed Issue on Public Management, vol. 69, Spring.

Ranson, S. (1990) *The Politics of Reorganising Schools* (London: Unwin Hyman).

Redcliffe-Maud, Lord (Chairman) (1969) *Royal Commission on Local Government, Vol. 1*, Report, Cmnd 4040 (London: HMSO).

Rhodes, R. (1981) *Control and Power in Central–Local Government Relations* (London: Gower).

Rhodes, R. (1986) *The National World of Local Government* (London: Allen & Unwin).

Richards, P. (1973) *The Reformed Local Government System* (London: Allen & Unwin).

Ridley, N. (1992) *My Style of Government* (Glasgow: Fontana).

Robinson Committee (1977) *Remuneration of Councillors: Vol. 2: The Surveys of Councillors and Local Authorities* (London: HMSO).

Robson, W. (1966) *Local Government in Crisis* (London: Allen & Unwin).

Rogers, S. (1990) *Performance Management in Local Government* (Harlow: Longman).

Rosenthal, S. (1991) 'Putting People in the Driving Seat', *Local Government Chronicle*, 6 September, pp. 20–21.

Rowbotham, S., Segal, L., and Wainwright, H. (1979) *Beyond the Fragments* (London: Merlin Press).

Sakwa, R. (1989) 'Commune Democracy and Gorbachev's Reforms', *Political Studies*, vol. 32, pp. 224–43.

Saunders, P. (1980) *Urban Politics: A Sociological Interpretation* (Harmondsworth: Penguin).

Scase, R. (1991) 'Dinosaurs in the New Organisation', *Financial Times*, 25 November, p. 15.

Scotsman (1993) 'Colleges Take Up Their Position in the Marketplace' (news report).

Scotsman (1993b) 'Labour Official Brands Councillors Meddlers', 22 May.

Scott D. (1990) 'The Last Word in Consumer Friendliness', *Scotsman*, 26 September.

Scott D. (1992) 'An Innovator with Public Interest at Heart', *Scotsman*, 11 June, p. 14.

Scottish Office (1992) *Devolved School Management: Guidelines for Progress* (Edinburgh: Scottish Office).

Scottish Office (1993) *The Government Expenditure Plans 1993/4–1995/6*, Cmnd 2214 (London: HMSO).

Selim, G., and Shaw, M. (1992) 'The Manager Monitored' in L. Willcocks and J. Harrow (eds), *Rediscovering Public Management* (Maidenhead: McGraw-Hill).

Sharpe, L. J. (1970) 'Theories and Values of Local Government', *Political Studies*, vol. 18, no. 2, pp. 153–74.

Sinclair, A. (1989) *Public Sector Culture – Managerialism or Multiculturalism?* (Melbourne: Graduate School of Management Working Paper).

Skeffington, A. (Chairman) (1969) *People and Planning: Report of the Committee on Public Participation in Planning* (London: HMSO).

South Somerset District Council (1992) Job description for policy review officer.

Stanyer, J. (1976) *Understanding Local Government* (Glasgow: Fontana).

Stevenson, J. (1984) *British Society 1914–45* (Harmondsworth: Penguin).

Stewart, J. (1983) *Local Government: The Conditions of Local Choice* (London: Allen & Unwin).

Stewart, J. (1971) 'The Personnel Function', in J. Stewart, *The Responsive Local Authority* (Birmingham: INLOGOV).

Stewart, J. (1974) 'The Responsive Authority', in J. Stewart, *The Responsive Local Authority* (Birmingham: INLOGOV).

Stewart, J. (1986) *The New Management of Local Government* (London: Allen & Unwin).

Stewart, J., and Clarke, M. (1987) 'The Public Service Orientation: Issues and Dilemmas', *Public Administration*, vol. 65, no. 2, pp. 161–77.

Stewart, J., and Ranson, S. (1988) 'Management in the Public Domain', *Public Money and Management*, vol. 8, no. 1, pp. 13–19.

Stewart, R. (1991) *Managing Today and Tomorrow* (London: Macmillan).

Stewart, J., and Stoker, G. (1988) *From Local Administration to Community Government*, Research Series, 351 (London: Fabian Society).

Stewart, J., and Stoker, G. (eds) (1989) *The Future of Local Government* (London: Macmillan).

Stoker, G. (1991) *The Politics of Local Government* (London: Macmillan).

Stoker, G. (1989) 'Creating a Local Government for a Post-Fordist Society: The Thatcherite Project', in J. Stewart and G. Stoker (eds), *The Future of Local Government* (London: Macmillan).

Strathclyde Regional Council (1976) *Regional Report* (Glasgow: The Council).

Strathclyde Regional Council (1992) *Report and Accounts 1991/92* (Glasgow: The Council).

Straw, J. (1988) News report, *The Guardian*, 23 March.

Sweeting, A. (1993) 'A Fair Cop, Guv?', *Guardian*, 18 May, p. 32.

Taylor, F. W. (1947) *The Principles of Scientific Management* (New York: Harper).

Tayside Regional Council (1990) *Management Paper No 1 – Strategic Management* (Dundee: The Regional Council).

Thomson, R. (1991) 'A Stranger on the Train', *Independent* 20 October.

Times, The (1993) Report, 1 February.

Tomkins, C. (1987) *Achieving Economy, Efficiency and Effectiveness in the Public Sector* (London: Kogan Page).

Torrington, D. Weightman, J., and Johns, K. (1989) *Effective Management: People and Organisation* (Hemel Hempstead: Prentice-Hall).

Travers, T. (1986) *The Politics of Local Government Finance* (London: Allen & Unwin).

Wainwright, H. (1987) *Labour: A Tale of Two Parties* (London: Hogarth).

Walker, D. (1993) 'When Minister Becomes Manager', *Local Government Chronicle*, 21 May.

Walsh, K. (1988) *Marketing in Local Government* (Harlow: Longman).

Ward, S. (1988) *The Geography of Interwar Britain* (London: Routledge).

Wheatley, Lord, (Chairman) (1969) *Royal Commission on Local Government in Scotland*, Report, Cmnd 4150 (Edinburgh: HMSO).

Widdicombe, David (Chairman) (1986a) *The Conduct of Local Authority Business: Report of the Committee of Enquiry into the Conduct of Local Authority Business*, Cmnd 9797 (London: HMSO).

Widdicombe, David (Chairman) (1986b) *Research Volume I: The Political Organisation of Local Authorities*, Cmnd 9798 (London: HMSO).

Widdicombe, David (Chairman) (1986c) *Research Volume II: The Local Government Councillor*, Cmnd 9799 (London: HMSO).

Widdicombe, David (Chairman) (1986d) *Research Volume IV: Aspects of Local Democracy*, Cmnd 9801 (London: HMSO).

Widdicombe, David (Chairman) (1986d) *Research Volume III: The Local Government Election* (London: HMSO).

Will, J. (1991) 'Chartered Streets', *Local Government Chronicle*, 17 May, pp. 15–16.

Young, K., and Davies, M. (1990) *The Politics of Local Government since Widdicombe* (York: Joseph Rowntree Foundation).

Young, K. (1987) *Politicians and Professionals: The Changing Management of Local Government* (Luton: Local Government Training Board).

Index